LEFT

Ryan Peters

LADY JUSTICE
PRESS

LEFT

ISBN: 979-8-9866869-0-5 (paperback)
ISBN: 979-8-9866869-1-2 (ebook)
Library of Congress Control Number: 2022914165

Printed in the United States of America

A man lies faceup in the dark predawn of the Mojave Desert. Hands bound behind his back, legs bound together, he's covered in bleach and blood. His penis has been brutally sawed off. "Somebody, please help!" Mary Barnes screams into the cold blue sunrise. She's blindfolded, in pain, and walking aimlessly toward the highway. They have just been assaulted by a stranger who is demanding a million dollars in buried treasure. From murdering his best friend to high-speed chases, breaking out of prison, and cold-blooded guile, this is the story of international fugitive Hossein Nayeri, as told by Lieutenant Ryan Peters of Orange County.

* * *

CONTENTS

Part IV
Closing the Net

Part V
The Trial

INTRODUCTION

*M*y name is Ryan Peters.

When I think about all of the cases I've worked on and all the justice that has been served—this one stands out the most. This is the story of how we arrested international fugitive Hossein Nayeri. It's bone-chilling and crazy-making. For the true crime enthusiast, there are multiple plot twists that I hope will keep you turning the pages. But this is much more than just a good story.

I feel like it's an important tale to tell because of how it affected my family and my community and how it turned an entire county upside down. This case drew a lot of attention and notoriety, but you haven't heard the entire story. The real story is in the details. The true foundation for the spying, poisoning, cheating, beating, kidnapping, torturing, lying, manipulation, and, of course, love is always found in the details. Why did this all happen? Why did they think they could pull this off? Why did they truly believe there were millions of dollars buried out in the desert? Why did they pick Michael—loveable, sweet Michael?

Details are what separate the good criminals from the average. Details are also what separate the good detectives from the average. I'm here to dive into the details.

Before we get started, I want to give you some context and background on my life. First and foremost, I'm a husband and a dad. My wife and I met at a youth group and dated as teenagers. When she went off to college, I trained to become an emergency medical technician (EMT) with a group of friends. Our mutual goal was to become firemen together. Answering 911 calls and saving lives was a thrill, but part of me knew I wanted to do even more with my life. It felt like there was some greater call for me to answer.

I remember the exact moment when the lightbulb went off about what my higher purpose would be.

There was a shooting at a house in the California community of Diamond Bar. As EMTs, we were staged close to the incident, but the cops were the ones in the thick of the scene. They were making the arrests, saving lives, negotiating, and handling the emergency head-on. I remember sitting on the curb, catching the intensity of the situation as it escalated. Voice levels were rising. I was feeling so close but so far away from being able to do anything to actually help. I realized: *I don't want to be on the sidelines, waiting for the emergency to be over. I want to be involved in the rescue. I want to be part of the solution before there is ever any need for an EMT.*

That was the moment my life took a new direction and shifted from firefighting to detective work.

I was accepted into the Long Beach Police Academy, where I clocked many long hours and graduated in 2002. It was an exciting time in my life when the Long Beach Police Department picked me up as a twenty-one-year-old rookie.

I was young, but I got criminal law enforcement experience under my belt quickly. From the onset of my new career, I began dealing with gang shootings, robberies, domestic violence, street prostitution, and lots and lots of drugs. Routinely, it was a fast-paced workday filled with arrests, foot pursuits, vehicle pursuits, use-of-force arrests, and, of course, the occasional taco cart lunch.

Long Beach was significantly different from my hometown in San Bernardino county. The daily barrage of violent crimes was eye-opening, and I had to think about my future in law enforcement. In Long Beach, it would take up to ten years before I could be promoted to detective and would require me to be working, boots on the ground, all of those ten years in the state's most violent areas. Instead of going from one horrendous crime to another for years on end, I wanted to find a community where I could really make a difference. I knew I wanted to advance my career and sink roots somewhere that needed me. If I'm honest with you, Long Beach just didn't feel like a place I wanted to be for the rest of my life.

In 2004, I heard about a job opening with the Newport Beach Police Department. This community was quite different but in a good way. The piers, the boat-filled harbors, and the expensive lattes were all very glamorous in contrast to the work I was doing with inner-city gangs. I applied with very few expectations and was offered a position at the bottom of the ladder. What felt so right at first quickly had me questioning myself. Within the first month of training in Newport, I wanted to go back to Long

Beach. Watching for stop sign violators didn't offer the feeling of making a difference that I experienced handling high-level emergencies in Long Beach. I was humbled.

Fighting violent crime was one thing but fighting the thieves and narcotics in Newport was going to be a whole new challenge. I quickly realized I was given an opportunity to learn a whole new level of the craft of investigation, even if it meant working traffic violations for a while. I began to see how the hard work of understanding the intricacy of the criminal mind was going to be attractive enough to stay committed to Newport.

In 2005 I was on patrol when I ran back into my wife-to-be, Ashlee. As mentioned early, we were high school sweethearts before she went off to college and I began my career as an EMT. But now, a few years later, here we were.

On this particular night, I had been called to a local bar on Newport Boulevard for a bar fight. While in the parking lot, as I was restraining the drunken suspect, I heard a group of women yell my name. As I looked up, I saw them in the bar line giggling and pointing at Ash.

We didn't talk that night as she shuffled into the bar, and I took a guy to jail, but with that quick glance,

I knew I needed to reconnect with her. A few days later, we decided to meet up—or what she calls our "Second First Date," where we went to dinner and grabbed drinks. I knew that night it would be her and me forever. Less than a year later, we were engaged.

As I write this, we're approaching our fifteen-year wedding anniversary. We have four kids—three are biological, and our youngest was adopted through the foster care system.

Our youngest daughter was born addicted to meth and heroin. We maintained ten hours of weekly visitation with her birth mother for twenty-two months until a judge terminated her parental rights. We learned a lot during the foster care process—most importantly was understanding how to exist within so much uncertainty. For nearly two years, we had no idea if this little girl we'd brought home from the hospital would be ours forever. Each time the social worker showed up or called, there was always the possibility that she would be leaving us.

We met her birth father, who was incarcerated during the foster care process before he was deported to India. When we visited him in jail, he was so respectful and appreciative of our love for his daughter. We exchanged phone numbers, and he reached out to us once he arrived home in India. We've maintained a relationship via video chat and text.

This was on the heels of the Covid pandemic, and it took another year for us to actually adopt her. She was born in 2017 and officially became ours a little over three years later.

While my wife's stress and anxiety were higher than ever as she shuffled between school, visitation, jail visits, home visits, and the kids' sports, this experience ended up being one of the most rewarding experiences of our marriage. Though the uncertainty of losing our daughter was ever-present, we were continually reminded that even if we lost her, we'd still have each other—and as long as we had us, we would be okay.

As a lieutenant, I don't have a normal schedule. This has been difficult at times, but it's a sacrifice our family makes for the higher good of the community. I'm typically at the office from 6:00 a.m. to 4:00 p.m. and then immediately shift gears into husband, coach, and dad in the afternoons. I want you to get a feel for how normal we are. Our weekends and evenings are filled with sports, and our summers are filled with family road trips, fishing, camping, swimming, and spending time with grandparents.

We are very active in our church community and neighborhood. My wife and I have hosted Easter egg hunts and hot chocolate Christmas caroling, and we volunteer our time with concerts in the park and political events.

We have a dog we rescued from the shelter and two rabbits from neighbors who convinced our kids that we should have them. Yes, I'm a cop, but I'm also a typical dad who plays "guess what animal I'm thinking of" and can't say no to fuzzy bunnies. I absolutely love coaching my kids' teams and creating time for date nights with my wife.

Over the last twenty years, I've found the best place for me to make a difference—raise a family and be involved in our community—has been working with the Newport Beach Police Department, the heart of where this story takes place.

I became part of our SWAT team in 2005, advanced to sergeant in 2013, and was promoted to lieutenant in 2020. I have overseen our field training program, as well as our jail. I have managed SWAT, K9, detectives, motors, traffic investigators, parking control, animal control, and our animal shelter. I was a detective at the time I got the call to work on the Hossein Nayeri case in 2012.

During this chapter of my career, we faced several high-level, highly publicized cases, one of which was centered on Nancy Hammour, whose body was found lying face down under the Newport Bay Bridge on Labor Day of 2013. I was the lead detective at the time the young mother had been shot to death by the Mexican Mafia. It was our job to find the murderer. And we did. But when I'm handling a case, I always wonder what people were thinking or how they got here. Think about it. *What if you knew your beloved family member was somehow at odds with the Mexican Mafia? How far would you be willing to go to safeguard their life? How hard have you already worked to get them sober, or right their wrongs for them, or put them on the straight and narrow? How many times do you have to put their well-being before yours or your family's? Is there a "line" when it comes to someone's effort level?*

Before that, the Chadwick murder hit in 2012, just two weeks after Michael's kidnapping. In this case, we had an Orange County husband and wife who went missing, only to find out that the British-born millionaire husband had staged the kidnapping and strangled his wife to death in their Newport mansion. Because of his wealth, he was able to bail out of jail and flee the country. We couldn't find him for years. Working together with multiple law enforcement agencies, his family, and various media outlets, we finally found him in Mexico and were able to make an arrest.

Fast-forward to one more example: the Dirty John case. The justifiable homicide of John Meehan, who had stalked, conned, and terrorized his wife's family before being killed by his stepdaughter, has been shared through Netflix and podcasting platforms that have attracted a worldwide following.

Again, what were people in this family thinking? How many times did they blow off his antics as "that's just him" or ignore the signs because it only affected them and didn't affect anyone else in the family? When you read or watch true crime, I hope you have the ability to ask yourself the hard questions and think about what you would do or how you would help a friend. People are typically too close to see the big picture.

I've been involved with multiple high-profile cases with the Newport Police Department, but nothing—nothing—compares to the case of Hossein Nayeri and the attack on Mary Barnes and Michael Simonian.

Let's start from the top.

PART I

The Investigation

CHAPTER 1

O *ctober 2, 2012.*

I was on a SWAT call last night. An armed man held his girlfriend hostage for hours before turning the gun on himself and pulling the trigger. Around seven o'clock in the morning, I'm driving home exhausted, attempting to restore myself by taking notice of what was otherwise a typical morning in Newport Beach—the beauty of a clear sky reflects in the glassy Pacific, the calm anticipation of the day in the faces of people out for a morning jog or sipping fresh coffee. My head is clear, and as I pull into my driveway, I'm ready for a nap.

Just as I've fallen asleep, I hear the phone ringing. It's my sergeant on the other end of the line. I have to go back out. There will be no sleep today.

As it turned out, there was no sleep for the next two years.

Early this morning, 137 miles away from the crisp coastal air, Kern County Sheriff's Deputy Steve Williams was driving alone on State Route 14 in the middle of the Mojave Desert. He was on his way to work when he came upon Mary Barnes, a Newport Beach resident. Mary was walking along the road, looking like a bloody mess, wearing pajamas, wrists bound and holding a knife. She looked frantic. Something was majorly wrong with this picture. So Deputy Williams pulls over and starts to untangle what exactly has happened.

* * *

Mary Barnes is a fifty-three-year-old white female, five feet six inches, and 125 pounds. A bit of a drifter, Mary was single for a long time before meeting and dating William "Bill" Bannon in Florida. She didn't have a clear life direction, was struggling financially, and became enamored with the idea of the Newport Beach lifestyle that Bill represented. So she began working for her boyfriend, Bill, selling timeshares, and moving across the country to live with him and his twenty-eight-year-old roommate, Michael.

Their four-bedroom house, a block from the beach, is everything Mary could have hoped for in relocating to the West Coast. She doesn't have any friends or family in the area, but that's okay—she's optimistic, romantic, enamored, and hopeful. Mary has fallen in love with her new life. She has no idea there might be a dark side to the men she moved in with, and she knows nothing of their marijuana empire being grown right under her nose.

Newport is still fresh and exciting to her. According to Mary, October 1, 2012, was a normal Monday night in her new life. Bill was out of town, which was not unusual. Mary hadn't seen much of Michael that day, but come to think of it, she hadn't seen much of Michael at all. Exhausted from unpacking, Mary fell asleep in her room somewhat early. When Michael came home, he fell asleep watching television on the couch on the second floor.

At 2:30 a.m., their peaceful night quickly turns into their worst nightmare.

* * *

Michael Simonian is a twenty-eight-year-old white male, five foot seven, 175 pounds. You would have no idea how wealthy Michael is by looking at him. And I mean that in a good way. He's an out-of-shape marijuana enthusiast with an entrepreneurial mindset who likes to take care of his family and friends. Picture a younger Zach Galifianakis, a slightly unkempt teddy bear that you can't help but love—oh, and makes lots of money. He has a girlfriend that is probably out of his league and two loving parents. He stays at his parents' sometimes, his girlfriend's sometimes, and rents a few rooms off-record around Orange County. He drives an older model Toyota—nothing flashy.

Michael grew up in the area. He knows how to grow a weed business. He makes about $150,000 a month and is constantly reinvesting his cash in marijuana equipment or new grows. He realizes he's being used here and there and often finds himself footing the bill for friends. He's a charming teddy bear of a people-pleaser. Even though some have tried to take advantage of his niceness, he never puts himself in a position to lose out financially.

Michael can't deposit his money from his medical marijuana business in a bank because, even though the business is legal in California, all marijuana is illegal at the federal level, so he operates his life in cash. Michael originally met his roommate Bill at a poker party. He likes gambling, likes Bill, and decides to rent a room from him. Why? Bill is good with a cash-only, under-the-table deal that doesn't put anything in Michael's name. Bill gets some extra money, and Michael gets somewhat of his own space when needed. It's a win-win.

* * *

The Attack

When we sort through Mary and Michael's initial interviews, we learn that Mary wakes up to a cold metal barrel of a gun on the back of her neck. A masked man has broken into their home. He blindfolds her and says, "This is not about you." The assailant tapes her mouth shut, zip-ties her hands behind her back, and then zip-ties her ankles together. As she's carried downstairs, she hears her roommate Michael fighting for his life. She is terrified. She feels helpless. She *is* helpless, actually. She can't move or speak or scream. She can't see what's happening. Full of innocence, having no experience with the dark side of life, she has no idea the terror she's about to endure.

On the second floor, another masked suspect wearing gloves strikes Michael in the face with the butt of a shotgun. Michael and the intruder struggle violently over the shotgun. The suspect begins hitting and ruthlessly kicking Michael, who is still resisting and putting up a good fight. Then a person-sized shadow on the wall increases in size as a second intruder enters the room. Michael's heart sinks. This is starting to feel impossible.

Suspect number two strangles Michael from behind. Michael struggles and still attempts to fight off his attackers, but as he begins to lose air, he feels weak and starts to faint. During the attack, the intruders are asking Michael—and only Michael, never Mary—one question:

Where's the million dollars?

Michael is mystified. He says he has $2000 in a sock in a drawer in the room. They can have it. But that's not what the attackers want. They are looking specifically for one million dollars, and they are not taking anything less.

Michael gives in to his attackers. He's lying limp on the floor when they blindfold him and zip-tie his hands and feet together, just like they did to Mary. They duct tape his mouth closed.

Michael is pulled feet first down the stairs, his head hitting every step. Mary hears all of this and is utterly baffled. Neither Michael nor Mary know who the intruders are or why they are being targeted— maybe they got the wrong house? Neither of them has a million dollars. *Does Bill?*

The sound of a vehicle pulling up creates new panic for the victims. Reality sets in—this is not a robbery; it's a kidnapping. The two masked men shove their human cargo in the back of the vehicle and get in the back with them. A third criminal is driving.

Michael is getting thrashed and thrown around in the back of the vehicle while being beaten. They tell him, "Be good, so you don't get this girl killed too." He can feel blood trickling down his face. He's kicking, moving, flinching, and at times the blindfold slips down enough for him to catch a glimpse of what is happening. In one of these moments, he sees a flash of black and white plastic that he immediately identifies as "panda paper." In the marijuana business, panda paper is used to reflect the light and enhance the harvest. *Are these guys some kind of hitmen from a marijuana Mafia?*

They drive an interminable amount of time toward some destination—which turns out to be a remote area of the Mojave Desert approximately 100 miles away. Mary is hunched against a wall in the back of the vehicle, hearing the brutal beating. She can feel slick plastic and cold metal with her hands that are still tied behind her. She is terrified and tries to disappear into the blackness behind her blindfold, tries to close her ears against Michael's horrific screams, tries to hold her breath against the stench of his blood and something else that smells like burning skin.

All the while, Michael is being tortured right next to her. The two thugs take turns maniacally singing: "Where's the million dollars, Michael? Where's the million dollars?"

Where's the million dollars?

* * *

Maybe I won't die, Michael thinks.

From his periodic glimpses of them, the attackers have their masks on the entire time. They call each other nicknames from *Reservoir Dogs*: Pink and Brown. They don't want to be seen or identified. So if the attackers can't be identified, Michael thinks it's possible they won't be killed.

But for Mary, the fear of death creeps into her bones. There is no mercy in any of this that Mary can sense. During the drive, she thinks her new roommate is dead for long minutes at a time . . . until he screams from some fresh new torture that Mary cannot fathom. She molds herself into the shape of the metal corner of the truck.

After one long silence, Michael suddenly reveals that he has $100,000 in a safety deposit box. It only serves to invite a new round of beating with something that feels like a lead pipe and with curses that they know he buried "it" in the ground. They insist with certainty that they know the million dollars is not in any bank. Still not getting what they want, the bad guys threaten to break bones one at a time—in the bodies of Michael's parents and girlfriend. It's clear they've been watching Michael and his loved ones.

For Michael, the physical and mental brutality throughout the drive exceeds the bounds of hell, both real and imagined. For Mary, the insanity of the experience brings on anger fueled by fear.

The car slows down and makes a turn. Mary hears the crunch of gravel underneath the tires. Something inside her fiercely determines it's not over. She decides that she doesn't want to die. Not like this. Not tonight.

The door of the car opens. Still bound and gagged, Mary and Michael are dragged onto the cold desert floor and laid out on their backs. From the sounds of Michael's jagged breathing patterns, Mary senses they are about two feet apart.

Michael jerks violently away from the attacker, who is all of a sudden right next to his face. In a graveled voice, the attacker whispers: "This is your last chance, you poor bastard. Where is the million dollars?" Michael, exhausted and broken, solemnly whispers back: "There is . . . no . . . million dollars."

That's when things get worse.

Mary hears the *glug glug glug* of something being poured, splashing over her roommate. *Is it gasoline? Are they going to set him on fire? Are they going to set us both on fire?* The smell is overwhelming. A toxic chemical is permeating the dark morning air. It's not gasoline, she realizes. Michael is being doused in bleach.

One of the attackers pulls down Michael's pants and puts his foot on Michael's chest, while the other one places a zip tie around Michael's penis and scrotum. One of them takes a serrated knife and starts sawing Michael's penis off while psychotically singing, "And back and forth, and back and forth." The cutting lasts forty-five seconds to one minute. After his penis is cut off, Michael is screaming and writhing in agony. He's coughing, choking on his own spit, and gasping in pain.

One of the attackers leans over Mary and touches her with the knife they just used. What are they going to do to her? Fear floods every cell in her body. She feels incredibly vulnerable—no one knows where she is or that anything is wrong. No one can hear her if she tries to scream. She can't hear any sound from Michael anymore. She doesn't know if he is dead or alive.

"It's your lucky day," one of the attackers says. "If you can find the knife, you can save yourself." The kidnapper drops the knife, and the three of them drive away as the sun's first rays begin to peek into the cold, dark morning.

Left for dead, Mary is in shock. She uses her knees to push her blindfold up enough to where she can see. Still bound, she manages to find the knife tangled up in a cactus. *It's a miracle.* She cuts her leg straps and stands up. She attempts to cut her wrist straps but can't because of the swelling.

Next, she tries to cut Michael's zip ties, but due to the inflammation and bleeding, she isn't able to free him at all. *Will the attackers be coming back? Are they watching her now? What just happened?* She takes the gag out of his mouth. Michael takes a deep breath and whispers, "That feels so much better." He's alive. *For now, anyway.*

* * *

It's a normal Tuesday morning for Sergeant Steve Williams—until it's not. He's had enough sleep, his coffee tastes great, and the morning radio show host is playing a decent mix of music and news. It has the makings of a perfect day in Kern County. But Sergeant Williams is a seasoned deputy, and his sixth sense is always alert. He knows what goes up must come down—that perfect mornings don't always turn into perfect days.

Throughout this story, you'll see several "God moments" take place. From brilliant investigative decisions, being at the right place at the right time, finding that perfect piece of evidence, making a timely and life-changing phone call, to having the right cop at the right time.

This is one of those moments. Right cop . . . at the right time.

Out in his peripheral vision, Sergeant Williams sees a woman stumbling around on the shoulder of the highway. He notices her hands are tied. She is in pajamas, seems exhausted, and is bleeding. She's holding a knife. *What the hell?*

Sergeant Williams pulls over to the side of the road. He has no idea the magnitude of this moment. As seasoned as he is in picking up on clues and working cases, Steve could not anticipate the heinousness of the story he is about to hear.

As a professional, his first step is to take pictures of her bound hands to document the situation. A younger, less experienced cop would have unbound her, cut her ties, and tried to get her medical treatment immediately. But Williams takes all the proper precautions. He looks at the situation from an investigative standpoint and safeguards all evidence.

Officer Williams: How long have you been out here?

Mary: I guess it was just before sunrise. Officer, my friend and I were kidnapped in Newport Beach. They threw us in a van. It happened so fast.

Officer Williams: What's his name?

Mary: Michael. He's in the desert, up the hill in the mountains; we need to save him. He needs help badly. I'm afraid he might not make it. Please, hurry.

Once the initial evidence is collected properly, Sergeant Williams calls for backup and medical support. Mary collapses into the patrol car with him and directs them as best she can. Her body has gone into shock, and she's shaking while she's trying to show Williams where to go. She has no idea if the attackers are coming back, nor if Michael has died alone out there. The ache of knowing she could have saved Michael is creeping into her consciousness. A new sense of urgency washes over her. They drive off-road to a gate, then a gulley, and finally reach the abandoned Golden Queen Mine.

Historically, much treasure is buried in the Soledad Mountains and the Mojave Mining District. The Golden Queen Mining Company produced over $10 million in gold and silver from 1894 to 1942. The area isn't exactly known for being crime-free. In fact, quite the opposite—the mine has attracted shady people wanting to strike it rich for over 100 years.

Sergeant Williams helps Mary out of the car, and they start walking to find Michael. It's 8:00 a.m. The mountains are back and to the right as they approach the crime scene. The sun is carrying on with the business of rising as though nothing has happened. A new day is dawning anyway.

As they walk further, the stench of bleach and blood becomes overpowering. They are definitely going in the right direction. Before they see Michael, they hear him groaning. This is good news. It means he's still alive. There's still a chance that he will make it.

* * *

I'm the lead detective when the call from Williams comes into the station: "We have two people from Newport who were kidnapped and left for dead in an abandoned gold mine." This situation is what has pulled me out of my bed and back into the field. From Williams's brief outline of the crime, neither Michael nor Mary can identify their kidnappers. Our job is to figure out who has done this and why. There are no leads, no ideas—there is nowhere to start. I'm briefly updated and gather my thoughts as I head to the crime scene at the house.

The awareness of the brutality comes into focus as the officers on-site in the desert begin to look for Michael's severed penis. If they can find it, they can reattach it, but unfortunately, it is nowhere to be found. The attackers had taken it with them purposely to ensure a lifetime of suffering. I can only imagine the devastation this will cause if Michael survives.

On the morning of October 2, 2012, we sent Detectives Freeman and Carpentieri, some of our best detectives, to interview Michael and Mary at the hospital while others research the victims' histories. We want to know their phone numbers, their relatives, their friends, and anything we can find in our databases about Michael and Mary. Our team, haggard from the night before, is fixated on reviewing video surveillance from local businesses and city parking lots. They are searching every single license plate in a four-block radius as we try to put together some of the puzzle pieces of this heinous crime. We are looking for something, anything, as a starting point to unravel this case.

I know I need to start the investigation from the inside out. That's why I'm starting at the original scene of the crime. It's important for me to walk through the house where Mary and Michael were kidnapped with crime scene investigators (CSI) to pick up on clues and get some initial data.

Mary's suitcases are full of clothes, open on the floor as I survey the crime scene. *She was still getting settled in at the time of the kidnapping.* I'm making notes as I do a walkthrough of the house:

- I notice Bill's car is in the garage, which is located off the alley.

- I notice the house doesn't look ransacked.

- It looks well kept.

- Expensive jewelry is still present.

- There's a small safe that can easily be carried, left on scene.

- There is no damage to the door, no damage to the windows, the front door and side door are locked, and the garage is closed.

I'm thinking: *This is someone familiar to them. This is someone familiar with the house. They locked up as they left.* Did they have the keys? Did they get the keys from Michael or Mary? Where was the car parked if there was already a car in the garage? It's not big enough for two cars . . . if a suspect vehicle was parked in the alley, how come nobody saw it? Where are the cameras? Why did they hide bloody sheets on the third floor? Who's lying about not knowing these guys? Is Michael lying? Mary? Someone had to have seen something . . .

As a next step, I want to meet with Sergeant Williams, and we plan to meet in his office to review their evidence. It's brisk on my drive over to Kern County. I'm about 100 miles north of Los Angeles, driving through farmland. Even though we're just west of palm trees and paradise, the county seat has one of the highest crime rates in the United States, with a violent crime rate of one in every twenty-one residents. This area is also known for its riches in gold, oil, and agriculture—which includes carrots, potatoes, lettuce, and watermelon. And, of course, the booming marijuana empires.

The Kern County sheriff's deputies give me great data immediately. We are trying to get as much evidence as we can, as quickly as possible. They show me photographs and footage of how the victims were found and give me everything they have. Nothing is held back. I'm impressed and pleased they have documented everything so well, but it's still an empty case. The evidence doesn't give me a direction.

* * *

At the hospital, Mary and Michael are beginning the slow process of physical and emotional recovery. Mary is unstable in her ability to recall information. We don't want to cloud things for her further by sending a male detective to question her, so we make sure a female detective is tending to Mary throughout the process. But she is not opening up to us yet, and she is not communicating well.

I go into Michael's hospital room. It's as bad as I think. His shoulder and wrist are severely injured. He's been beaten, torched, mutilated, bleached, and—blindsided. The trauma is very fresh. He's confused, angry, and in a lot of pain. In his mind, he has no enemies. He has no idea who could have done this to him. He doesn't know anyone capable of this level of cruelty. But I know better.

The culprit has got to be someone who knows him, someone who has been watching him, and someone who knows exactly how much money he has.

I just need to break some ground with him so that he can trust me.

There is a five-hour delay between the first interview he gave Detective Carpentieri and the time I arrive. There's a sterile busyness in Michael's room. He's being asked a lot of questions between treatments, new IV bags, and fresh dressings on his wounds. I know he's already been through so much, and I hate feeling like I'm bugging him.

My main goal in meeting with Michael today is to establish trust, that I'm working for him. I want him to know, like, and trust me so we can work together to get to the bottom of this as quickly as possible. I don't want to ask him a bunch of additional questions right now. I'm just here, showing my face as someone on his side. But instead of talking openly, he's argumentative. Michael insists that he has no idea how this could have happened. He wants me to stop asking him questions and start finding his attacker. It's killing me that I'm not getting through to him.

The attitude Michael is giving me is understandable. After all, he's working in a very "gray" profession that doesn't have the best rapport with cops. Sure, selling medical marijuana in dispensaries in California is legal in 2012, but he also knows that I know that he's buying illegally to survive as a company. I remind him I'm not looking to charge him with anything, in any way, shape, or form, nor will I be charging him in the future. I'm only here to try and find who did this to him so that justice can be served. We want to protect him, his family, and the community from the monsters who did this.

But throughout our conversation, Michael is angry. It's hard for him to remember the details, and he's getting more and more combative. I remind him I'm trying to shine the light on any past experiences, associates, or arguments he may have had.

Michael finally mentions Bill, the owner of the house where he was attacked. He met Bill during a high-stakes poker party in an affluent community. A buy-in would cost each player $25k to $100k on any given night. They would bring in cocktail waitresses, have a massage therapist rubbing their backs while they were playing, and there would be large, expensive Vegas-style tables, lots of food, and lots of drinking.

While Michael is telling me this, I remember that we had a SWAT call to one of the poker parties where Bill was playing. At that party, three armed males broke into the house, beat people up, and robbed them. One escaped, but we caught the other two. We rescued the homeowner, and everyone else made it out safe. This was about a year ago.

I decide to keep the conversation brief, knowing I'm not getting any different information than the detectives obtained earlier. I tell him I'm going to be relentless for him. I need to convince him that what he has endured is not random. There's a reason behind this brutality. I tell him it's my job to figure out who did this to him—and to put an end to it.

Everyone is a potential suspect, and everyone is a potential victim. I need to talk to Michael's parents and girlfriend. They have to know something that will be helpful in breaking this case. So at the end of our interview, I ask Michael for a list of his family and friends that I can interview. I ask him to give them a heads up that I'll be calling. Even in homicides, witnesses and families are reluctant to talk to police. People get really nervous and hesitant with law enforcement. I need their full cooperation, and that begins with his trust.

I am confident the flow of truth will come out slowly, drip by drip. We have to be persistent and patient.

Michael's parents are open to talking to me. I get the feeling right away his parents are not involved in the crime. They are worried they could be a potential target. I begin to wonder: Does the dad owe someone money, or is he in trouble with someone who has retaliated and hurt Michael? I promise Michael's mom that we aren't going to drop the ball on this. I tell her as much as I can without scaring her, and I assure her we will find out who did this and put them in jail. I give her my personal cell phone number and allow her to call or text me anytime.

There's no immediate evidence against the parents, and there's no vibe or gut feeling I get when I'm around them. So I help Michael's dad set up private armed security at their home and facilitate Michael's girlfriend staying at a hotel with some friends in Palm Springs. We do this to continue to push the "trust door" open wider, but I'm getting nowhere fast.

I leave the hospital with no definitive information. No ideas. No leads.

Even though I'm growing frustrated, I fully trust our team. All hands are on deck. We have over a dozen experienced detectives working the case, collecting statements, researching data, and watching surveillance tapes. Everyone is investigating every possible lead, and this means our resources are draining quickly.

Back on the road, I'm tired. Our entire team is ragged, especially the SWAT team that has been working for three days straight with me. I update my wife and check in on the kids. Everything is okay at home. I continue sorting through possibilities for what could have happened in my mind, filtering all of the data that has come in today. *Who did this, and why? Where are they now? When will they strike again?* I'm going home, and I'm going to review the evidence all night.

CHAPTER 2

*I*t's the next day. I haven't slept that great, but I'm ready to get some more traction on this case, so I decide to go to the place where the bodies were dumped. I want to be there at the exact time I believe the crime happened so I can get a feel for what clues might surface.

At 6:30 a.m., I get out of the patrol car at the Golden Queen Mine and begin walking the path that Mary walked—toward the highway. This gives me context for understanding what she was going through. I want to hear what she would have heard, see what she would have seen, and get a sense of what happened.

The far-off buzz of morning traffic seems distant. Only a tiny sliver of highway is visible in the dark morning sky—and that's without a blindfold. I'm convinced there is no way she could have seen the highway at all. This explains why she didn't take the shortest route to the highway, completely missing the actual road that was used by the suspects.

There is cactus everywhere. It's rough terrain. This would have been a very difficult walk under normal circumstances. But bound, gagged, and scared to death, I imagine Mary was in shock and just putting one foot in front of the other. She must have felt the terrible pressure that Michael's life—if he was going to make it—was in her hands.

I can still see the footprints and tire marks, and I can still smell the bleach in the area Michael was found. The air is cold and crisp. The hillsides make it impossible to gain a perspective as to where I'm at in relation to the highway. I can only think: They didn't really want Michael and Mary to be found. They didn't leave them here believing they were going to make it. They left them for dead. And I don't see how they thought they were going to uncover buried money. I'm surrounded by desert, and every ten feet is identical to the next. How would anyone believe someone is actually burying money out here? This is insane, and the story doesn't make sense.

Information from the other detectives is flooding in. I go back to my car to sift through the texts, calls, and emails. I pull up Senior Deputy District Attorney Matt Murphy's number on my phone. His cell rings twice before he answers.

"Hey—we've got a crazy one," I tell Matt as soon as he says hello.

I proceed to tell Matt the pertinent details of the case. Just the bullet points. I know we don't have what we need right now—I'm just keeping him aware of the situation that's unfolding. There's no suspect, no compelling lead to investigate, and no clues strong enough to form a lead. Murphy has won over 100 jury trials at this point in his career. He hasn't lost a single case since 1996. I realize I care a lot about that record, and I don't want to let Matt down. I'm not going to bring him anything less than an airtight case. I don't want to let myself down either—and I can feel the pressure building to figure out what has happened and why.

Then my phone rings.

A detective calls with a piece of information that changes everything.

PART II

A New Lead

CHAPTER 3

*N*ewport Beach is easily one of the West Coast's most beautiful beaches, a place where surfers, yachters, and sunbathers congregate to let the azure ocean waves wash away their worries. It is easily one of the wealthiest cities in the United States. The average home here costs well over two million.

Fine dining and upscale shopping opportunities dot the peninsula with lavish, high-end lifestyles. On Balboa Island, you can paddleboard with whales and dolphins and then grab an iconic frozen banana from Sugar 'n Spice, which has been around since 1945. It's idyllic. Picture perfect. Luxury, elite experiences with large, expensive cocktails in hand—there's a reason Newport Beach's 65,000 residents love it here.

On any given day, there is a very low chance of being involved in a crime of any kind. In fact, there's an average of less than four violent crimes per year in Newport Beach, making it feel like a pretty safe place to live and travel. The general vibe of the American Dream is one of the main reasons why we decided to raise our family close to this area.

Statistically, there are very few murders in Newport Beach, less than one per year. More common are the occasional drug crimes, vandalism, or random theft—not a calculated kidnapping at the level of brutality we've just experienced with Mary and Michael. It's not normal for intruders to mutilate victims looking for buried treasure. It's terrifying. This kidnapping is a major crime anywhere, but it's very unusual here in Orange County.

So as the word on the street spreads about this horrific crime, one of Michael's neighbors spills some solid information to one of our detectives. In fact, it's the key that turns the ignition on in this case.

The detectives call to update me on their conversation with the neighbor and other evidence they are finding. I'm now driving as fast as I can back to the crime scene. My thoughts are racing with what little nuggets of information we have so far.

What else did Michael's neighbor see? Is she our only witness?

The detectives found someone suspicious walking eastbound on Balboa on security camera footage, about thirty minutes post-kidnapping. Is it related? Is this one of our guys?

We saw sheets unusually placed in the third-story attic of the crime scene. Why?

Why wasn't Michael sleeping in his bed the night of the kidnapping?

What the hell happened here?

When I get to the scene, Michael's neighbor is extremely scared. She fully believes these guys will come back to get her. She's being very cautious as she explains what she saw.

She says something suspicious happened outside of Michael's home the day before—*the day of the crime.* She had been in her upstairs bedroom when she heard a truck pull into the alley and stop. Keep in mind the alleys are extremely narrow here. There's only about twenty to twenty-five feet from one beach house to the next. So when she looks out the window and sees three men in their alley that afternoon, she is able to see everything clearly. It's daylight, she's sober, and this is really happening.

One of the men she sees is wearing a hard hat, and one of them is carrying a ladder. There are no other tools. Nothing else stands out—but something seems off to her. They don't look like painters, lawn servicemen, or construction workers. She hasn't seen them before. She watches the three guys walk around Michael's house as if they're looking for something or scouting it out. They're looking suspicious without actually working on anything. This is taking place around 3:00 p.m. on the day of the crime.

If these three men were the culprits, they had been in the house the entire afternoon waiting for Mary and Michael to come home and fall asleep. You're telling me they were lying and waiting for hours without truly knowing what they were going to find in the house during that time? You're telling me they weren't worried about someone else coming home? They weren't worried about being seen or heard or if a house cleaner came in? Did they know the inner workings of the house? Did they know there weren't any cameras in here? Or did they just get lucky?

This is her nightmare—to come home to a house full of kidnappers, fall asleep innocently, and then be attacked in the middle of the night. She knows Michael well enough not to be scared of him. She has only seen Mary a few times. But her concern is very valid: If this type of thing can happen to them, what's to stop it from happening to her?

The neighbor is paranoid and doesn't want to be involved in the case at all. But being a good neighbor, she wanted to share what she saw with law enforcement. We believe she is a credible witness at this time. Then she gives us the big news—the piece of data that is the turning point in this case.

She gives us the license plate.

We run it.

The truck is owned by Kyle Handley of Fountain Valley.

We finally have a real lead.

* * *

I head back to the station to reorient the team. The truck and plate give me what I need to confidently narrow our search.

Scattered efforts become draining over time—when no one is able to keep us pointed in a direction. So as long as we have one objective, one mission, and one direction, this will keep morale high. This license plate is the focus that will keep everyone motivated to keep working on this crazy case.

Seasoned SWAT officers leave to work surveillance on Kyle Handley's house, about fifteen miles into Fountain Valley, while I look through all of our databases for information on Kyle, his truck, his house, and any basic information. We need to figure out who this guy is and what his level of participation is in the kidnapping.

Kyle Handley is thirty-three years of age, five foot eight, 165 pounds, and a white/Asian male who looks Hispanic. He's a normal-looking, unassuming kid who grows marijuana and sells it to local dispensaries like the ones Michael owns. He's from Fresno, which is near the area where the bodies were dumped. So far, there's just nothing special standing out about Kyle.

I'm thinking: Okay, so he's in the same business. This kid doesn't have a record, doesn't look like a stone-cold killer, and doesn't physically look like he can carry it off. I can't wait to peel back this onion and find out more on this one.

We know he's renting a house in his name, and his name only—the electric bill is through the roof, which confirms he's likely been growing pot recently at that house. This is not a surprise since we know he has tickets for illegally selling and growing marijuana on his record. This gives us some clues but doesn't give us enough evidence to pull a search warrant.

The team in Fountain Valley calls me with some immediate news: they see a camper shell on a white truck in the driveway in front of Kyle's house that matches the description and plates of the truck the neighbor has associated with Kyle and with the kidnapping.

This is huge.

Right now, we know there *was not* a camper on the truck when the helpful neighbor reported the truck and license plates with the three mysterious men outside of Michael's home. We also believe, based on Michael and Mary's statements about the back of the vehicle used in the kidnapping, that the vehicle could have been a truck with a camper shell—and now we have Kyle's truck with a shell on it.

Just as we get a burst of energy in the case, the sun is beginning to set. It's nightfall, and the SWAT team is still lingering at Kyle's, undercover, without a warrant. We don't have much, but it's something, and I'll take it.

While surveilling Kyle, the detectives see he's the only one home. He's playing video games, smoking weed by himself, and walking around the house nervously in circles.

It's pretty spartan there. There's a couch and TV in the living room and a Ping-Pong table where a normal dining room table would go in an otherwise unfurnished home. From the outside looking in, there is no obvious evidence that would link Kyle to the kidnapping, besides, of course, the truck. But we're getting close.

The California skies are completely dark now, and Kyle is getting more restless. At 10:00 p.m., he gets in a two-door Nissan that's been parked in his driveway, leaves the house, and drives to a warehouse in Long Beach. Two detectives on the team follow him to the warehouse, but they lag behind so they can stay unseen. Once Kyle is done at the warehouse, one detective stays there to figure out which storage unit is Kyle's, while the other detective follows Kyle back home.

Something's up.

I feel confident Kyle's been involved somehow. We've got testimonials from the victims, the camper shell, the neighbor/witness, and now suspicious late-night activity in the warehouse. So I write a warrant asking for the opportunity to search Kyle's car, his warehouse, his person, and his home in an effort to link him to the kidnapping and brutalities associated with Michael and Mary.

It's well into the night on October 3 when I drive to the presiding judge's home in Costa Mesa. He reads and signs the warrant just after 2:00 a.m. *Knowing I've got the warrant in hand relieves the whole team, but we have a long way to go and many more twists and turns to make with this case.*

The next step is to call the county task force to come relieve our Newport officers, who are totally spent. The county guys are fresh and ready to tag team with us. They are able to sit on the house and continue surveillance while we get some much-needed rest.

I'm fading hard. I have to get some rest in order to stay sharp for Michael and Mary and their families. I spend what feels like the next forty hours sleeping. But there's one man who won't get any rest that night—and that man is Kyle.

CHAPTER 4

The next day the county team checks in with an update that Kyle didn't go to sleep at all. They say he seems nervous and scared. He's chain-smoking cigarettes and puffing weed from a bong. He's playing video games nonstop.

We agree there is no need to jump the gun in our approach to searching Kyle. We don't see other people in there, but we don't know for sure if he has any hostages or how dangerous he is. We're all just waiting for Kyle to leave the house so we can study his next move. We need Kyle to give us more. We need him to show us who his associates are, where he likes to eat, and where he likes to hide evidence.

We're going to use Kyle as a building block in this case. So we're going to wait.

We don't wait long. Late that night, the phone rings.

It's the task force.

Kyle leaves his house and heads toward the 7-Eleven.

"Find a reason to pull him over," I tell them. The county task force team pulls Kyle over for a vehicle code violation, and I fly over there as fast as I can. He has illegal knives in the car and is under the influence. Good news for us. Bad news for Kyle.

The knives and intoxication alone give me a reason to detain and arrest him, but these are completely different charges than the ones that have been brewing.

I walk up to Kyle's car and see him as a scared kid. He's pale, sweating, and much more incredibly nervous than someone should be—who, in theory, was simply pulled over for a vehicle code violation. He knows exactly what he has done, and he looks as guilty as he must be feeling. I ask him to get out of his car, walk him back to my patrol unit, and read him his rights. I ask if he knows why I'm talking to him. Before I can say anything about the knives or intoxication, he lawyers up. *"I want to talk to my lawyer."*

It's going to be like that.

So while Kyle gets booked on the knife charge at Newport Police Department, I drive over to his house, where CSI are working diligently. We start documenting the outside as a first step. We video the perimeter of the house. We are very slow, methodical, and thorough—taking nice, steady, safe steps.

Next, we go to the truck and open the door. Immediately it reeks of bleach. The foul chemical smell is disgusting, but it's a little reward. It's an acknowledgment we are following the right lead. And, honestly, it's our first indication we are going to get these guys.

It's clear that the back of the truck has been cleaned up, so we focus on the front cab area. We see one blue nitrile glove on the floorboard. Immediately CSI buttons up the truck and tows it to our garage at Newport Police Department for further investigation and DNA testing.

In the house, we are still moving slowly and meticulously. I'm spending thirty to forty-five minutes in each room, documenting everything, questioning everything. There's a little bit of weed and some remnants of an electrical cord in the attic where he was likely growing marijuana at some point. There's only one bed, barely any clothes in the closet. Not much to show so far . . . until I see it—a black shirt with bleach droplets all over it stands out like a blinking neon sign.

In the laundry room, there's a clear plastic container that has some zip ties in it. In fact, they are the exact type of zip ties that we cut off Michael and Mary when they were rescued in the desert. There's a growing feeling that Kyle is definitely associated with the kidnapping.

At this point, on the outside, I'm a professional investigator searching a house for key pieces of evidence. On the inside, I'm a kid on Christmas morning standing at the top of the stairs anticipating with great excitement what's downstairs under the tree. I can barely hold in my excitement. I can feel the evidence starting to solidify.

We go to the garage and continue the investigation. There's a four-foot roll of panda paper—the same black and white plastic paper used in marijuana grows—that fits the description of what Michael and Mary had seen at moments during their kidnapping.

Each room gives us more and more clues. We are getting more and more excited—everything's adding up. But right now, a bunch of clues is all we have. It's not enough evidence to charge Kyle with the crime. I keep the DA updated every moment. He tells me we are on the right track, both of us wanting more solid evidence. So we continue searching the property.

Outside in the backyard, we see several black trash bags that are mostly full. Our CSI team is videoing as a detective begins pulling out the contents of the bags. He drags some bleach-covered, red-stained towels out of the first bag and lays them on a piece of butcher paper. He rubs a chemical over the stains and determines it is, in fact, blood. We save this for DNA testing.

What happens next is the moment we've been waiting for.

The next bag we open is neon green. Inside it is a zip tie that has been tied closed and then cut. During the kidnapping, Michael had reported that he was complaining about his shoulders and arms. He said that one of the guys who wasn't beating him came over, cut the zip tie, and put a new one on him. Fast-forward to the present moment, and I'm standing with a cut zip tie in a trash bag of bloody and bleach-soaked towels at the home of Kyle Handley—the man whose truck has been placed at the scene of the crime and the man we now have under arrest.

Kyle Handley is in it up to his neck. On October 6, 2012, Kyle's charges change to kidnapping, mutilation, mayhem, and aggravated assault. But who the hell is Kyle Handley, who are his associates, and how the hell do they know Michael Simonian?

CHAPTER 5

O n October 7, we search Kyle's warehouse in Long Beach. I'm praying and hoping we find actual evidence of this crime. I'm looking for things like bleach, blood, property belonging to Michael or Mary, and any evidence of who else was connected. We know we are looking for a minimum of two other people who were there for the kidnapping, but we have no idea how big of an area the spiderweb of this crime encompasses.

In the warehouse, there is marijuana-growing equipment: lighting, tubing, buckets . . . but nothing else. I find an address of a second warehouse Kyle has in his name in Long Beach and take the search there. This one is an open warehouse that is a 10,000-square-foot shed on cement. He's paid rent there, and the electricity bill is also in his name. It's dry. I leave empty-handed.

I'm reviewing the timeframe in my mind. We know Michael fell asleep around 10:00 p.m. and that Mary had fallen asleep before he did. She was in her room with the door closed. He's on the couch sleeping in the room next to his when the assault happens. At some point, he's woken up, beaten, and kidnapped. Neither Michael nor Mary know how long they were in the car. We know how long it takes to drive from the house to the desert, but we don't know if they drove straight there. We know the drive is long and traumatic, and we know that the detective finds Mary early the next morning.

There are some pretty big gaps and a lot of missing information, but with the stuff we have on Kyle . . . it's more than we had yesterday. It's a start.

It's time to look into Kyle's family next. He has an older brother who is squeaky clean—a real estate agent who lives with their parents in the same house where Kyle and his brother grew up. The parents seem normal. They are furious we won't give them the blue Nissan. It's registered to them, and, naturally, they want it back. Of course, we can't give it back because we need it as evidence. So I'm not making many friends at the Handley household. This road seems to be going nowhere—I've got to find another outlet to learn more about Kyle's past and why he would be involved in something so heinous.

It doesn't make sense to reach out to the weed collectives in Orange County because none of them will want to tell us where he's been selling or who he is associated with. But there is someone who *will* give us this information . . . Michael Simonian.

I drive back to talk to Michael, who is staying under armed security at his parents' house. I show him a picture of Kyle Handley. A look of disbelief washes over his face.

"Yes, that's Kyle. Yes, I know him."

* * *

Nearing the end of October, Michael is still staying at his parents' home, recovering under armed security. His mom is calling me almost daily for reassurance and an understanding of where we are in the case. One day, I'm at a pumpkin patch with my kids, and her number pops up on my personal cell phone. As I'm staring at the phone, the look on my face must be indicative of what I'm thinking because my wife has a quick and stern response.

"Answer it," she says. "If I were his mom, I'd want you to answer."

So, at the request of my wife, I sit in our car during our family outing to talk things through with Michael's mother.

As I sit on the phone, staring off and watching my family run around picking out pumpkins, I'm listening to a grieving mother. Sure, she didn't lose her son, but she's emotionally upside down. She doesn't know who to trust, doesn't know who to turn to, and doesn't know what advice to listen to. She's lost. She isn't truly confident in trusting everything her son is involved in, and she doesn't know the current threat level toward him or her, for that matter. She is scared and looking for guidance. Let's be honest—she also wants to vent. She wants to be heard; she wants someone to be empathetic to her feelings. She's looking for someone to tell her it's going to be okay. She knows I have most of the information surrounding this case. She trusts that I'm going to be honest with her, and I have been to a certain extent. She knows she can be honest with me too—and that's worth something.

I talk with her for about thirty minutes and then return to my family.

I am really growing fond of Michael and his parents. I feel for them during this tragedy. He's a loveable guy, and I'm getting angry on his behalf. *Who did this to him, and why?*

Michael's healing process is as physical as it is emotional. He is in and out of several cosmetic surgeries to rebuild his anatomy back to functioning. Over time, he opens up to tell me more of the background story, including his relationship with Kyle Handley. They developed a friendship through Michael's company, Right Green. And while I am beginning to get a picture of Michael's point of view of their relationship, I see a much more sinister plot had been developed a long time before the actual crime. And Kyle isn't "just another suspect"—he's a real player in this horrible act.

Six months prior, in early 2012, Kyle and his associate approached Michael about selling some marijuana they've grown at the house in Fountain Valley. They bring in a sample to Michael at Right Green and attempt to start a relationship with him. After all, Right Green is one of the largest and highest-selling legal dispensaries in Orange County, and anyone in the weed business wants their product represented here.

Michael says the weed doesn't meet his expectations and turns them away based on quality. Seemingly undeterred, Kyle becomes a regular buyer at Right Green and starts hanging out with Michael.

Michael says he likes Kyle and becomes his friend—Michael even invites Kyle on his birthday trip to Las Vegas with his girlfriend, other associates, and business partners. At Michael's expense, they rent a huge suite for $10,000 per night. Michael pays for sexual favors for Kyle and tries to show all of his friends a good time over the course of the weekend through generous spending, partying, and gambling.

As we find out later, unbeknownst to Michael, Kyle was tracking Michael's every move over the course of several months.

All we know at this point is that Michael remembers Kyle as a buddy—a friend in the industry. We also know that Kyle is somehow connected to the kidnapping. But keep in mind that we don't know the extent of Kyle's underhandedness yet.

And we have yet to learn of the other associate in this heinous crime—the puppet master pulling the strings.

PART III

The Puppet Master

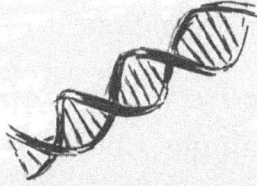

CHAPTER 6

*O*ver the next several weeks into November and December 2012, we continue to work the case with everything we've got. We meet with Michael at his parents' house, showing him maps, directions, and pictures of where he was found. But he isn't emotionally ready to help with the investigation at the level we really need.

It takes Michael a long time after the incident to break through the trauma to remember he actually *had* been to the Silver Queen Gold mine before. What Michael remembers about the mine starts with meeting a Russian guy who was a customer at Right Green. The Russian pitches investing in a mining operation to Michael and ends up driving Michael out to the lot in Silver Queen.

This feels hot for investigation.

We take this lead and serve warrants to be able to look through the Russian guy's house. We are thorough in looking through every single piece of property he owns. We follow him for about a week and a half. Turns out, he's just a pot-smoking scam artist who has nothing to do with the crime. Another dead end.

If I'm honest with you, I'm pretty frustrated. It's been several months since we started, and we are dead in the water. We are waiting for a return on the items we collected from Kyle's house and sent to the crime scene lab: Kyle's truck, Michael's clothing, the zip ties, everything. But since we don't have a homicide, we are not a priority with the crime lab. So we wait.

* * *

Finally, a DNA match comes in from the rubber glove we found in Kyle's truck. This is an arrow pointing us in the direction we need to be going, but it doesn't tell us whose DNA this is exactly. We know it isn't our victim's, and it isn't Kyle Handley's. *So whose is it?* Another month goes by before we get a name.

On January 7, 2013, I learn that the DNA on the glove belongs to a fugitive named Hossein Nayeri. I've never heard of Nayeri and know nothing about him. Michael doesn't know him either. So I've got to research this guy in all of our local and state databases. *Game on.*

Nayeri first appears in our records just six days before Michael was kidnapped and mutilated. The record states that on September 26, 2012, a driver evaded the Newport police while driving a Chevy Tahoe in a high-speed chase that ended at Balboa Island. There, the driver got out of the vehicle, jumped into the harbor, and was never found. No one is apprehended, but the Tahoe is confiscated. *This is just about a week before the kidnapping.*

Another one of those God moments is Officer Maisano being in the right place at the right time; he's one of the hardest-working officers we have in the field.

When he impounded the Chevy Tahoe, he found two cell phones—an Apple iPhone and an AT&T flip phone—which are booked into evidence. He didn't find drugs, guns, bombs, or anything crazy and decided to leave it in the tow yard. Pretty routine, considering we're investigating a felony evading suspect.

After the chase, the officers notice Hossein is linked to a Cortney Shegerian at an address in Newport Beach. In the records, she isn't married, has a different last name, and uses different bank accounts. Definitely fishy.

So after the chase, an officer goes to Hossein and Cortney's home in the middle of the night and speaks with Cortney. In a sleepy state, she confirms that, yes, Hossein had the Chevy Tahoe that evening, but she doesn't know where he is right now. As she's talking, her facial expression shifts from confusion to agitation. It dawns on her that something isn't right. In fact, she's starting to realize something is seriously wrong. Cortney gets defensive, becomes uncooperative, and refuses to answer additional questions. She will not give the officers Hossein's phone number or any leads on where he might be. She doesn't seem to be concerned that the car is wrecked and that Hossein is missing.

The next day, Cortney calls our office and reports the vehicle as "stolen." She's told that the Tahoe is impounded for investigation. The driver of the Tahoe, during the night of the chase, is still outstanding, and the police department is holding onto the vehicle during the investigation. She insists she'd like to have it back. But our officers are suspicious. They remind her she confirmed her presumed husband had the vehicle and denied her the return of the car. They tell her they will need Hossein's statements on his whereabouts before they are willing to turn anything over.

Fast-forward to the present moment: January 2013. After receiving the confirmation that Hossein's DNA was in the glove, I have to know more about this couple. I send a team to surveil Cortney and, hopefully, Hossein. As their story unravels, Cortney moves to an expensive high-rise apartment in Santa Ana off the Costa Mesa freeway.

While the team is watching her, I fill out a search warrant for the impounded Tahoe and go back to the evidence records to search the Tahoe more thoroughly. I find documentation that Hossein is on the insurance of the car, that Cortney is the owner, and that they are both linked to the original Newport address. In the vehicle, I find two small hidden security camera devices and a mini GPS tracking unit.

What I find next is shocking, and it connects Hossein to the crime.

CHAPTER 7

*H*ossein Nayeri is a thirty-three-year-old Iranian male, five-foot-ten, and weighs 190 pounds. He's got a muscular, thick athletic build, but nothing over the top. He has black hair and brown eyes and comes off as charming. Much later, we will find him to be a maniacal, sadistic, egotistical, narcissistic, manipulative sociopath whom prosecutors would later refer to as "Hannibal Lecter."

Nayeri has been in trouble many times during his thirty-three years. Born in Iran, he came to Fresno, California, as a young boy without knowing any English. His dad is a doctor, his mom is an attorney, and he's the middle child.

In high school, Nayeri got into many fights. He was active on the wrestling team.

At age twenty-four, he enlisted in the marines and was quickly upgraded to a position in surveillance because he was so cunning. During his two-year service in the marines, he continued to get into fights, he stole, and he went AWOL. Hossein was given a dishonorable discharge which he fought in court to change to "discharge" and won. It goes without saying that the marines didn't work out for him.

So Nayeri returns to Fresno and works as a waiter in Mimi's Café, where he sees Cortney Shegerian. Cortney, sixteen, found Nayeri funny, magnetic, and intriguing. He's charming and seems to really get her. They begin a relationship that she has to hide from her parents. She's only sixteen when Nayeri begins to court her. Her father, a prominent figure in Northern California, would never allow his daughter to date an older male. She is spending a lot of time hanging out with Hossein and his friends—Ryan Kevorkian and Ryan's girlfriend, Naomi. She doesn't know what she is getting herself into as the relationship grows.

* * *

Back in the present moment—it's January of 2013. We are watching twenty-three-year-old Cortney closely. Months after the crime in which Hossein is now implicated, she's always by herself. She's going to and from law school, and that's it. She never works. Doesn't go to the gym or go shopping and never goes anywhere suspicious. She drives a brand-new car and just goes to school and home, school and home. When we ask the apartment complex if anyone else is on the lease, they say no—just her.

We begin tracking Cortney and Hossein's cell phones. We ping his phone and trace it to her apartment. So we write up a search warrant. We want to go into her apartment and gather more evidence. I'm trying to figure out how I can get her to talk to me, and I remember that back in October, she wanted the Tahoe back. So I devise a plan to give her what she wants.

However, by now, there is a little more to the offer to return the Tahoe. Remember the cameras I found in the Chevy Tahoe after the high-speed chase? What is on those cameras is a real game-changer.

* * *

The cameras confiscated from Hossein and Cortney's Tahoe reveal hundreds of hours of video surveillance . . . of Michael and Mary's home. They have been stalking them for approximately six months. On the phones, I find text messages from a GPS tracking unit, which include addresses for Michael's house and his parents' house. The GPS tracking unit had been attached to Michael's vehicle and was used to monitor his every move. They knew everywhere he had driven and everywhere he had been over the last several months.

Interestingly, I also find Cortney's number listed as a contact on Kyle Handley's phone.

At this point, I believe the suspects—Hossein and Handley and maybe Shegerian—took Michael and Mary to the Silver Queen Mine in the Mojave Desert because they thought Michael had hidden money in that area. After all, they would know—since they were in the marijuana business—that he wouldn't be able to put cash from marijuana sales in a bank and that he would need a place to hide unscrupulous income. We also know that *they know* that Michael had visited the Silver Queen Mine area (where the victims were dumped) in the month prior to the possible investment with the Russian. *That location would have been captured by the GPS tracker.*

During this process, I've retrieved all of the clothing in the Tahoe for further review. We find that one of the Adidas sandals we found in the car is actually visible in part of their surveillance footage, which links this sandal to this car and to Michael's house.

Here's where we are as of late January, early February 2013: We have Hossein Nayeri's DNA on a glove in Kyle's truck, the truck has been identified *by license plate* the day of the kidnapping at the scene of the crime, and there is video surveillance evidence of Michael's home (and a shoe from the car in the video) in the Tahoe owned or operated by Cortney and Hossein. Cortney, Kyle, and Hossein all knew each other from Fresno and are contacts in each other's phones. We have found zip ties, bleach, and other objects at Kyle's house that are linked to the crime scene.

Cortney will definitely be wanting the items in the Tahoe back. But how badly?

* * *

I call Cortney and tell her I'll give her the car and everything in it; she just needs to come down to the station to pick it up. She's game. Smiling when she arrives, I take her downstairs. Everything is laid out on a table: their clothes, the trackers, the phones. Everything. *As I explain every item on the table and how she can take ownership of all of it with a simple signature, I'm thinking there is no way. I'm literally handing her evidence to a maniacal, well-planned, gruesome kidnapping, and she's just going to sign for it and walk out. There is no way she'll do it.*

Without hesitation, she signs the release papers, grabs the stuff, and starts to leave.

Not so fast.

"Cortney, everything you have in your hands has been associated with a kidnapping. Are you aware of this?"

At first, she blanches and appears confused, then she's furious. Cortney yells, "You tricked me?! This isn't fair! Do you know who I am?! Do you know who my father is?!" She wants nothing to do with me and is not answering my questions.

I pause for a moment. Cortney is an inferno of anger. She's full of rage and defensive. But when I handcuffed Kyle, he looked like a scared little kid. *What do these differences indicate? Let's put a pin in that thought.*

We search her car, her person, and her new apartment, but we don't get anything new from Cortney. It's frustrating as hell, but it's not over. I vow to Michael and his parents that I will stop at nothing until justice is served. So I go back to my desk and continue researching. As you might imagine, the

Cortney and Hossein love story is full of angst and twists as we inch forward in the case.

One report states that when Cortney and Hossein lived in Irvine, she filed a domestic violence suit against him and then later backed off. In this report, she says that Hossein also beat up their best friend with a bat . . . that she was scared of him, terrified actually. There are other instances of domestic violence when Hossein has beaten Cortney, stepped on her neck, and even threatened to kill her.

Then I notice an entry in Nayeri's files that stops me in my tracks.

CHAPTER 8

*I*n 2005, Hossein killed his best friend. In the incident, Hossein, Kyle, and a third friend Ason Tusci were out enjoying a typical night of gambling, drinking, and dabbling in the marijuana business. Drunk, Hossein drives Ason's car home. He loses control, rolls the car multiple times, and his closest friend Ason dies on the scene.

Hossein limps away with some burns and loses some toes. But what he does next is very telling. He doesn't stick around to grieve, mourn, or serve justice. Facing a vehicular manslaughter charge, Hossein gets on a plane to South America. He stays in Argentina for a year and eventually sneaks back into the United

States, where he gets a reduced charge and is released from a local jail. *That's it. That's all the heat he got. Thanks to our solid justice system, Hossein is free again!*

Hossein is sadistic, elusive, and violent. If I know one thing about violent guys, it's that they are *always* violent—they never change. And he has a history of not being held accountable that dates back to his time served in the military. *He seems to get away with everything, and this pisses me off.*

Iran! Oh, I didn't mention that yet. He's in freaking Iran! While I'm trying to convince Cortney to take possession of evidence linking her to a kidnapping, my phone is blowing up from some of my federal friends. They found out Hossein jumped on a plane the second Kyle was in handcuffs and split. That motherfucker!

How am I going to get this suspect, an Iranian National, back from Iran and in custody in the United States of America? Oh sure, they'll just hand him over. Iran loves America.

Hossein—a killer with an abusive past—is gone again.

PART IV

Closing the Net

CHAPTER 9

*C*ortney Shegerian is twenty-six years old, five foot seven, and weighs 130 pounds. She has long black hair and big brown eyes. Cortney is unique. She is smart, witty, and highly ambitious. She is also lost, naive, and scared to be alone. She was abused by a family member early in her life and continues the cycle of physical and emotional abuse with her boyfriend Hossein, who also talks about killing her. She feels that he is all she has, and she keeps their relationship private. *After almost seven years, her family has no idea she's still with him.*

Hossein convinces Cortney to become a lawyer, and she uses the trust fund her father set up to pay for her school—and their wicked lifestyle. In fact, when Hossein fled to South America after the DUI crash that killed their friend, Cortney financed medicine and money for him for a year. Then he decided to come back and turn himself in.

Turns out Cortney is, in fact, married to our main villain Hossein. We know the couple attended the same high school as Kyle Handley—in different years, seven years apart—and that they grew up in the same town, Fresno. We know Hossein's sister lives nearby in Redondo Beach and has a positive relationship with Cortney. The phone records indicate that the sister is not talking to Hossein, *but she is talking to Cortney*.

* * *

After the disastrous meeting with Cortney at the station, I realize that I can't quit on her. Based on Michael and Mary's descriptions of their captors, I know she wasn't in the back of the car beating, mutilating, and torturing Michael. Yes, she's involved, but we need her on our side to get this job done. We need her to talk. I have no doubt that with Cortney on the witness bus, we can get to the bottom of things and catch the guys who kidnapped and maimed our victims.

As I sit at my desk, staring off into space, trying to make sense of all the evidence, characters, stories, lies, and next steps, it dawns on me. I'm a father that would do anything for his little girl. *I'm going to call her dad.*

Not wanting to screw this up, I run this idea by Deputy District Attorney Heather Brown, who is an absolute badass when it comes to prosecutions. She's relentless and brilliant in the courtroom, and I am blessed to have her on my side.

Mrs. Heather Brown is all in. She loves the idea. "Do it!" she says.

John Shegerian is the billionaire CEO of Electronic Recyclers International. When we connect on a call, he's thousands of feet above California on a private jet. I talk to him father-to-father for the better part of an hour. I tell him I'm a dad and that I would want to be fully involved with the situation if this were my daughter.

"I think you need to help inform and guide her through this, John. Her future is on the line."

He understands the implication of her involvement in criminal behavior will drastically affect her future and appreciates that I've called. Will she spend her life in jail? Or will she be an attorney living a normal life, putting the bad guys behind bars instead? The consequences are severe. He wants her to be in our good graces as soon as possible.

Within ten minutes of hanging up with John, I get a call from Lewis Rosenblum, a prominent lawyer who is suddenly representing Cortney. The attorney requests the DA's name so we can set up a proffer—a contract for providing useful information that won't be held against her. Within the hour, we have a date for Cortney to come in the following week for her to start talking to us about what exactly has happened.

Driving home that night, I'm filled with actual hope for the first time. I have Kyle in custody, I know Cortney was involved, and I know Hossein Nayeri is in Iran. Before Cortney agreed to a proffer, I was always missing something. There was always "more." More people to find, more evidence to secure, more places to search; I needed more. This need for more was daunting and draining. But now, having Cortney on the witness train, with a solid lawyer representing her and her family's emotional support—I finally feel real hope.

* * *

You know the saying, "In for a penny, in for a pound"? Cortney is in deep and needs our help as much as we need hers. She's facing the same sentencing and same guilty verdict as everyone else if she refuses to work with us.

The proffer is our ticket to mutual success. It is an agreement between the defense attorney and our department that Cortney will cooperate with the entire investigation. The DA verbally agrees to not use what she says against her based on how helpful she is. She swears in writing to be 100 percent truthful, and we are able to move forward.

It's a delicate situation. Neither party knows if they can trust the other. So I'm talking to her like she's a friend. I'm telling her things like, "You need to be strong. He manipulated you. We need to get you to a therapist; this isn't your fault." I'm trying to help her see that she's not this evil person that she has been led to believe she is and help her separate emotionally from Hossein. I'm a shoulder to lean on to motivate her to unshackle herself from the chains with this guy and set herself free.

Over the course of the next several weeks, Cortney and I talk three to four times a week to establish rapport, and her side of the story begins to unfold. When she relays the details of her direct involvement and admits she's as culpable as the others, I know we've got her on our side. This is data I can work with.

Cortney shares that she was attending Cal State Fresno in 2008 when she reconnected with Hossein. Their relationship is on again, off again. Hossein is emotionally abusive, insulting Cortney's appearance at every level. Tells her she's ugly, hates her nose, hates everything about her. He breaks her down and separates her from her family, all while conning her to pay for his lifestyle. She's alone and isolated in Hossein's dark world.

Their relationship becomes even more dysfunctional and toxic. The neighbors call the property manager to check on them because they can hear the fighting, and they can see the pushing and shoving. In one episode, he bites her arm so badly that her skin turns black. He throws her to the ground and puts his foot on her neck. Cortney says this type of physical abuse is a normal, weekly occurrence, but at one point, she calls the police.

She reports he's pinned her to the floor, put her in a chokehold, and threatened to kill her with a box cutter. She presses charges, but Nayeri is let off on a deal. He goes to anger management classes, and the case is dismissed. He doesn't get any jail time, and no domestic violence is on his record.

The more he gets away with, the more violent he becomes.

Cortney is living a double life. She's attending law school and is on her way to a respectable career. But at home, she's under the control of an abusive murderer. Fast-forward to 2011, when Kyle Handley, the man we've associated with the crime at hand, reconnects with Cortney and Hossein and moves in with them. Unbeknownst to her family, Hossein convinces Cortney to fund their attempt at a marijuana business in Long Beach. Hossein sees this as an easier path to make money—so they start growing.

Kyle and Hossein approach Michael to sell their product, but Michael is not interested. He doesn't approve of the quality. This infuriates Hossein. He takes great offense to this one single denial of a sale and immediately begins to calculate some rough numbers in his head. *Pompous douche.*

Hossein begins his plot. He buys burner phones, multiple laptops, surveillance equipment, and different outfits and starts log after log documenting Michael's whereabouts and a list of his friends, family, and associates. He's not leaving a stone unturned.

The plan is for Kyle to befriend Michael and figure out where Michael's money is ending up. Hossein is never directly involved with Michael, but he's watching and studying behind the curtain. They plant GPS trackers on Michael's car, his parents' car, and his girlfriend's car. They have video cameras on Michael's house, his parents' house, and on any commercial lot Michael associates himself with. The sim cards have to be replaced every twelve hours, so they are there frequently. The cameras are cheap, but they are getting the job done. They have video surveillance running for several months, getting a better sense of who Michael is by following his every move. *This is the evidence on the trackers that implicated Cortney and got her to talk to us.*

It becomes Hossein's obsession to track Michael. He's working on a plan to steal a million dollars from a guy he doesn't know . . . all because his product was rejected. One day, Hossein is sitting at the kitchen table and calls Cortney to come look at the tracker with him. As Cortney leans over to see it, he says, "Look. This guy is driving all around the desert. It looks like he's driving in an abandoned gold mine. I bet he's burying his money out there."

Cortney, not really wanting to argue with Hossein, says, "Sure. I guess he could be." From that moment on, Hossein is convinced. Michael's money has to be out there in that mine, and he's going to get it.

Cortney tells me everything she is directly involved with when it comes to Hossein's plan to steal Michael's money. She is the one who ordered the phones they used to track Michael. She is the one who bought the construction worker hat that was worn in the alleyway. She is the one who made the poison to potentially kill Michael's parents' dog if it became loud, in the event they would be confronting him and breaking in at that location. Kyle had left his car near Michael's house the day before they kidnapped him. Cortney was the one who moved Kyle Handley's car the day of the kidnapping so it wouldn't get a ticket in Newport Beach.

What she doesn't know is who Mr. Brown really is. She also didn't know the plan—that the three of them were going to hurt and torture Michael, much less cut off his penis. She didn't know where the guns came from.

Cortney does know Kyle and Hossein are in this together, and she knows a third male named "Mr. Brown" is part of the crime. She also knows the cameras and trackers were ordered under Naomi's name (Ryan Kevorkian's ex-wife), but she doesn't know the extent of Naomi's twisted involvement.

As we discovered previously in the investigation, Ryan, Kyle, and Hossein all grew up together, and at one point, Ryan and Hossein were best friends. Naomi and Ryan were high school sweethearts that eventually got divorced as adults. They were all one big happy family. Until they weren't.

Cortney knew Hossein talked to Naomi but didn't know how involved they were. During the first week of Cortney and I going over every little detail, I was the one who brought Naomi's name up. Cortney was caught off guard a bit. She didn't know Naomi was truly involved in this.

This brings us back full circle in the build-up to this story. We're still unable to bring this grisly and horrific case to an end, even with all this new data. The chief architect of the crime, Hossein Nayeri, is gone, and, at this point, we haven't identified "Mr. Brown" or spoken to Naomi.

We continue to dive into Cortney's dark past with Hossein, looking for more evidence to be able to apprehend Hossein and get a conviction. Their relationship and everything around it is laced with violence. In story after story, Cortney shows me that Hossein is always able to get out of whatever situation he gets himself into. He is a master at avoiding conflict and confrontation when it's directed at him. It's his pattern, and she's not wrong. No one chased him when he ran from the car wreck that killed his friend. No one chased him after he left the Tahoe and swam away in the bay. He just seems to get away with shit.

But someone's chasing him now—and I am not going to stop.

CHAPTER 10

*M*y next move is to obtain an Interpol warrant and reinsert Cortney in Hossein's life. I need him to believe she is still supporting him and isn't ratting him out.

In the early months of 2013, Cortney and Hossein start talking on the phone more often. The calls are recorded, but Hossein doesn't know that. I have got to know if she's really doing the job we've asked of her, so I hunker down and listen to hundreds of *hours* of their conversations. We're working to build his trust in Cortney that she's still loyal to him, and I'm still watching Cortney—making sure she isn't going to flip on me.

Meanwhile, back at the station, there's still a zip tie from the crime scene that has not been matched to anyone's DNA. I need the third suspect.

Every week Cortney meets me to hand over their phone conversations. We talk about her life. I'm interested in her emotional well-being, and I'm making sure she is sticking with the plan and that she still trusts me. I'm also making sure she is being honest with me. I need to know our relationship is becoming stronger than her current relationship with Hossein. I don't want this guy to convince her she still loves him. I need Cortney to trust the process, trust me.

Part of building trust, I know, is that it has to go both ways. To open up some of that trust, I update Cortney on where I'm at with the case. I let her know we are still searching for that third suspect. I try to make her feel like I'm certain I know who it is, but I'm dying for some concrete evidence to prove it. So with that information, she takes it upon herself to find out from Hossein. I know this isn't going to be easy.

* * *

Fast-forward to May 2013. Cortney calls and says she has some exciting news. She comes rushing down to the station to share her latest phone conversation with Hossein. *I've got a team player now.* As we play the recording of their call, I hear Cortney manipulate Hossein into talking about "Mr. Brown." I must say, it's pretty smooth how she gets him to do it.

In the call, Hossein describes "Mr. Brown" as coming through with "flying colors."

"You should have seen it," he says. "He was great! I knew there was no way Kyle was going to be strong enough to do it. I knew I needed to get some muscle. Someone I could actually trust."

Cortney is a natural at this. She's stroking his ego and edges in the question we've been waiting for: "Well . . . who is Mr. Brown?" Cool, calm, and collected, Hossein says, "Ryan." As if she should know which "Ryan" he was talking about. It just so happens she does. She says, "Oh! Ryan. I didn't know you guys still talked."

Hossein then rants about how he figured Ryan was down and out on his luck and could use the money, and on and on. In his sick mind, involving Ryan was a way for Hossein to make amends to their relationship, and he would be doing him a financial favor.

I ask Cortney who "Ryan" is. She says it's Ryan Kevorkian. *We have a solid lead for the third assailant.*

* * *

From May to September of 2013, the hunt is on for Ryan Kevorkian and his ex-wife, Naomi. Ryan is a Persian male, five-ten, 225 pounds, with a muscular build. Ryan and Naomi were high school sweethearts who have two kids together. They went to the same high school as Cortney and Hossein did in Fresno.

As our investigation unfolds, we learn Kevorkian's dad is a warden at the local prison in Fresno, California. He got Ryan a job as a custody guard after Ryan came home from serving in the military with Hossein. There at his job, Ryan cheated on Naomi with a female inmate who he was helping smuggle contraband into the prison.

Ryan's falling in love with an inmate put a major rift in the group's friendship. Hossein took the infidelity very personally and became extremely protective of Naomi. Hossein, who was married to Cortney at the time, took a baseball bat to his "best friend" for cheating. Hossein beat Ryan relentlessly in front of his house, and, again, cops were called, charges dropped, and everyone went on their merry way.

Looking back, we see this as another example of Hossein's great manipulation act. He's playing husband to Cortney and fill-in husband to Naomi at the same time. Hossein is secretly taking care of Naomi physically, emotionally, and financially behind everyone's back. Hossein felt a need to take care of Naomi's kids and spent a lot of time with her and her daughters but kept their "friendship" separate and private, similar to his secretiveness about his marriage to Cortney.

Per Cortney, she and Hossein have not talked to either Kevorkian or Naomi in years. As far as she knows, the last time they spoke to Ryan was during the baseball-bat-beating incident. Once we learn this history, we decide it's important to do some surveillance on Naomi as well.

The matrix of people involved is complex as to who knew what. *Let's recap.*

Ryan Kevorkian was unaware that either Naomi or Cortney was involved in the crime. Naomi didn't know that either Ryan or Cortney was involved. Hossein didn't trust Kyle with any information. Cortney damn sure didn't know Ryan or Naomi were involved. However, Hossein knows each one involved and controls the action like a puppeteer.

When Kevorkian is found out to be screwing the inmate, it is all over the local news. He gets fired and has nowhere to go. He's disgraced his father, embarrassed his mother, and has no job. But a month later, it's Ryan's lucky day. His fling is being released from prison and needs a baby daddy. Kevorkian moves in with his prison girlfriend and begins playing dad to her five children from different fathers. The happy family is all living in a one-bedroom apartment, where she is making ends meet by nannying, and he watches the kids. Oh, and they didn't make it far. They're still in beautiful Fresno, California, right by Mom and Dad.

* * *

We put a team on Kevorkian to follow him for a few days. Our goal is to capture his DNA and compare it to the zip tie DNA. The plan is to follow him into a fast-food place where he sits by himself. An officer will dress up as a restaurant employee and take his trash for him. We could bag it, process it, and capture his DNA. But Ryan never goes out to eat. He only goes to the gym.

So we focus on the gym. I work with some amazing detectives who know what we need, how to get it, and how to blend in. This "DNA Recovery" operation isn't easy, and it's not done on a daily basis. The detectives need to be quick thinking, adaptable, and clever, all while trying not to get caught. Everyone knows how big this case is, and nobody wants to be the person to screw it up. One of my detectives, Detective Perkins, is probably one of the best undercover detectives I've ever worked with. The guy is smooth, fluid, and confident—exactly who we need on the case.

While the team is in Fresno, we finally get lucky, and Ryan heads in for a workout. We put our best guy inside the gym with him—Detective Perkins. On the fly, Perkins is getting his pump on right next to Kevorkian. As Detective Perkins is watching him, he notices Kevorkian is using the same towel throughout his lifting session. Perkins quickly focuses on the towel and begins to figure out how to obtain it. Keep in mind that we can't steal it from him. It has to be something he gives up and makes no claim as his.

Kevorkian throws his towel down on the counter in the restroom and walks out. Detective Perkins quickly grabs the towel and takes proper precautions not to destroy any possible DNA Kevorkian may have left behind.

We get the towel back to the lab for processing, and our luck continues. The gym towel DNA matches the remaining zip tie that was in the back of Kyle's house. This evidence is what we need to serve warrants on Kevorkian, his girlfriend, and his ex-wife Naomi. *A small island of relief . . . maybe we can relax a little this weekend and take the kids to Mammoth. Get in some fishing, bonfires, and smores. Anything to get away and celebrate the small victories.*

* * *

Naomi Rhodus. Born in 1980, five-foot-six, 150 lb., with long blond hair and brown eyes.

In the summer of 2013, the investigation in Fresno is moving slowly, and we are focusing our efforts on filling in details about Naomi's involvement in the crime. We find Naomi's parents are taking care of her kids while she goes to work. It's moderately interesting that she bought a handgun last year. But what's *more* interesting is what's happening in the background.

When we served the warrant on Cortney's Tahoe and were going through information retrieved from the trackers found in the car, we were able to connect a name, address, and email address of who purchased the two cameras and the tracker. It was purchased by an email associated with Agriglobe, Inc. Where does Naomi work? You guessed it.

But at this point, Naomi is still protecting Hossein. Unknown to the others, Hossein has been helping

Naomi and her kids ever since she split from Kevorkian.

In late September 2013, we serve search warrants on Naomi, Naomi's parents, Naomi's work, Ryan Kevorkian, Ryan's apartment, and everything in between. Ryan immediately lawyers up, and Naomi thinks she's going to outwit us. She talks a little but mostly plays dumb. She thinks she's smarter than she is and isn't giving us anything we don't already know. Actually, some of the stuff she's giving us doesn't even make sense. She's trying to cover up for Hossein, and I have no idea why. *Why does she sound like she loves Hossein? Why is she protecting him so much and yet acting as if she doesn't even talk or communicate with Cortney? What the hell is going on with this group?!*

It's late September 2013, and I'm still working with Cortney. We're still building her and Hossein's relationship back up, letting them "bond" and fall back in love with each other. In the meantime, we have Ryan Kevorkian, Kyle Handley, and Naomi Rhodus in custody, and nobody wants to talk. We'll wait until Naomi misses her kids and wants to get out of jail.

In April of 2014, she calls uncle and wants to do a deal. She spills that she had a friend rent the U-Haul van that was used in the crime. She lied to the friend about why a van was needed and why Naomi couldn't rent it by herself. She swears the friend knew nothing and rented it for her innocently. In addition to purchasing the trackers, we learn that Naomi has assisted the three kidnappers by purchasing a handgun for them and providing the shotgun.

We also find out that Cortney wasn't the only one visiting Hossein while he was on the run from us. Naomi says she also met Hossein while he vacationed in Turkey and in Thailand to provide him with additional clothing and medication. *She's in this as much as anyone now.* True to form, Hossein totally lost it in Turkey, and, according to Naomi, he had choked her to the point where she thought she was going to pass out.

While we continue to question Naomi, Hossein is still out of reach. He knows he's in a safe place—that Iran is not an ally of the United States. He feels safe; however, he is unaware that we are building a case against him and that, sooner or later, we're coming after him.

The next step is to establish a working relationship with allied countries around Iran and set up an Interpol warrant to get this guy.

CHAPTER 11

After the brutal kidnapping, Hossein Nayeri fled to Iran just one day after Kyle Handley was apprehended.

How can we lure him out of Iran? The answer is right in front of me—we use his wife, Cortney, as bait.

I'm still listening to their private phone calls for evidence, tips, and clues. I'm still monitoring how truthful I think she's being. They talk every day for a few hours each day, and I'm going with my gut that these are honest conversations. Several times they allude to the crime, but the majority of their calls are about nothing. It becomes clear that he is beginning to trust Cortney with her calling him "just to say I love you."

In one of these conversations, Hossein randomly starts going off about the crime. He tells Cortney, "I made Kyle throw away the penis. He needed to be guilty for something because if not, he would be the rat. So I cut off the penis and handed it to Kyle. That little pussy was sick the whole way home. I made him clean up his throw-up while he was still holding onto the penis. Then I made him throw it away so he couldn't turn on us."

This is huge.

* * *

Hossein, of course, doesn't know that we have Ryan and Naomi in custody. We block off the ability for civilians to search their names in the Orange County jail. The three of them want nothing to do with Hossein, so we aren't worried about any of their family or friends getting in touch with Hossein for any reason. Nothing gives them away.

We've got Ryan, his girlfriend, Naomi, and Kyle, and now we just need Hossein.

In the calls I've been listening to, Hossein reveals he's missing Cortney. That's my cue that he's ready to meet up with her again. Time to plan a trip for them to meet someplace where I know the Interpol warrant will help me get him back to the states.

* * *

he International Criminal Police Organization, or Interpol, must be involved if we are ever going to get Hossein back to the states and convicted. We need to start the process by going through the FBI.

First, we have to create a state warrant that shows a vicious, violent crime took place in California. This documentation shows that Hossein is wanted and is on the run, which escalates it to a nationwide crime. So the FBI picks up the case. They adopt our warrant, create a stand-alone federal warrant, and collaborate with Interpol to recover an international fugitive.

Most allied countries are in agreement that an original violent crime in the United States is also considered a violent felony in their country. This means that almost all of our allied countries are able to help with an extradition.

With allied countries, each country has to create its own warrant. Since we aren't going to do that for all allied countries, we narrow it down to three—with

Cortney's help—that we think will make the most sense.

Cortney says that, when they were married, they had always wanted to go to Spain and Greece. While she butters Hossein up to meet in Spain, we reach out to our FBI agents in Spain, Greece, and the Czech Republic to create the first warrants for those countries.

Cortney: Hi . . . it's been ten months since I've been able to be around you, like every day, you know? It's just not what I envisioned. You didn't know I wanted to see you? I say I miss you every single time I talk to you; are you fucking joking? Let's spend a couple weeks together. Come on! We can travel all around Spain and do whatever; it'll be great.

Hossein: Spain, I hear, is a nice place.

Cortney: I want to see you. I want you to come and meet me . . . then we can be together, together forever (singing). I love you so much. I want to see you.

We are making several plans with international FBI agents in case he enters either Spain or the Czech Republic. In August of 2013, we obtain an Interpol warrant for fugitive Nayeri, along with individual warrants in Prague and Spain.

* * *

Meanwhile, Hossein is living the good life in Iran. Since he's been gone, he's received money from Cortney, Naomi, and his mom. He's spending time with his cousin going to bars and restaurants, and even traveling within Iran to go snowboarding and hunting. He fears no capture while in Iran—and why should he?

He does want to see Cortney, and he also wants to see his sister, Nadar. Cortney is still putting on a show for Nadar, keeping the relationship between them active, and goes so far as to attend Hossein's grandfather's funeral. Per Cortney, Nadar feels Hossein should not be on the run. She believes Hossein is on the run because of something Kyle Handley did and not her brother. She thinks him being gone is "dumb" and has no idea Cortney is in the middle of setting up her brother.

Cortney knows the trip would be much more believable to Hossein if Nadar were coming along. So Cortney sets plans in motion. We make another proffer with her and agree to turn a blind eye to whatever she's doing to help him get a travel visa. She creates a fake green card and fake visa so Hossein can travel and plants a seed with Nadar about the trip.

Cortney knows how to get the job done. She has contacts in Los Angeles and finds a guy to create fake documents for Hossein with his photos and a different name: birth certificate, social security card, driver's license, etcetera. She goes to a travel agent, knowing they will hand over the travel documents.

Cortney performs all of her tasks perfectly and gets the new identity documents over to Hossein. Now the ball is in his court. He fills out an application online for the travel visa under his new name, and it's game on.

There's a tremendous amount of nervous tension building up in the office. It's been a little over a year since Hossein and his criminal friends kidnapped and tortured Michael. Everything is riding on the proper execution. We need Cortney and Nadar to get on a plane in Los Angeles. We need Hossein's fake travel visa to work, and he needs to make his plane flight to Spain, which has a layover in the Czech Republic. I can't afford time for plane delays, bad weather, or planes rerouting. I need the grace of God and a bit of luck for justice to be served.

Here's how it went down. Once they have the official travel visa, Cortney buys plane tickets from California to Spain for herself and Nadar and the ticket from Iran to Spain for Hossein. His flight from Iran has a strategic layover in the Czech Republic where we have a good contingent of FBI agents .

. . and a warrant. He's suspecting nothing. Nadar knows nothing. *If this falls through, we're screwed.*

* * *

November 7, 2013. I'm waiting at home for the moment of truth with adrenaline coursing through my body. Cortney and Nadar land in Spain. They haven't heard from Hossein, and Cortney is freaking out. The night he's supposed to come, he's not answering her call. Eventually, he calls her back. He says he's sorry he overslept and that he will be there to see her very soon. *This guy better not screw this up. He better get his ass on that plane. He didn't figure it out, did he? He's not that smart, right?*

I'm constantly checking in with my FBI contacts making sure he got on that plane. They don't get the boarding information when he gets on the plane (obviously, Iran doesn't share that information with the rest of the world in a timely manner. But I did find out when he landed in the Czech Republic, during the customs check before he got off the plane).

So I'm excited . . . then I start letting my imagination get the better of me. I'm thinking, "What if he runs? What if they screw it up, and he gets on the plane to Spain? What if . . ."

Then I get the call.

He's in custody.

We've got him! Holy shit, it's over.

But it's nowhere near over.

* * *

Hossein is held in Pankrac Prison in southwest Prague. It's a 100-year-old dungeon that is wet and cold, with no hot water. They take his stuff, strip him, do a full body cavity check, give him their standard gray shirt and pants, and throw him into a dingy cell. The jail is a WWII prison that was built back when the Germans were invading. It's rusty, damp, dark, infested with rats, and everything he deserves.

Hossein is waiting for trial far, far away from Cortney. Even though she is nervous, Cortney is finally able to stop pretending. She stops communicating with Hossein and Nadar while waiting for the trial. She files for divorce and has their marriage annulled while getting her life back on track.

Hossein is waiting to be heard by a Czech jury regarding his fugitive status. If he wants to change his circumstances, Hossein has to give himself up for extradition *back to the United States* by waiving his right to trial in the Czech Republic. So, a year later, having suffered the rats and the misery of the foreign jail, he signs the waiver and is finally in the custody of our FBI.

* * *

The plane ride home.

The Czech Republic dropped its charges in September of 2014. They will no longer prosecute him for being a fugitive, and Hossein Nayeri is cleared for extradition to the US. The FBI takes him into custody and flies with him to JFK International Airport in New York City on September 9, 2014.

Standing in JFK awaiting his arrival, I can only think about what I want to say to him, and I'm wondering what he is going to say to me. He's been served with the documentation that shows I'm the one behind the warrant that makes him culpable for the whole thing. He's read the entire report I wrote.

He knows who I am.

When I see him emerge from the plane, he's walking casually down the ramp of the boarding bridge and into the terminal, ahead of the FBI agents. His shoulders are back, head held high. He's confident, moving at a normal pace. There is no sense of urgency or anxiety present in his demeanor. Once he sees me, he never takes his eyes off me. When he gets closer, I introduce myself.

"I'm Ryan Peters. I'll be taking you to Newport."

Hossein replies, in the most smug, arrogant, and deep voice, *"You're younger than I pictured. I've been reading your affidavit."*

That was it. That's all he says. All business.

I tell him to turn around. I take the FBI handcuffs off him and put my handcuffs on him. This is symbolic but also very real. My partner at the time, Detective Cammack, helps change his clothes and his ankle chains, and we proceed to the terminal that will take us to the next plane and back home.

There's a long line of people waiting to get on the plane. It's a commercial flight from New York to California. Everyone in line is staring at us. We can't help but draw attention. I can only imagine they are thinking, *"What the fuck. They aren't getting on this plane, are they? I'm not sitting near them."*

We board the plane first and immediately position ourselves in the back. Hossein sits near the window staring outside the majority of the flight. He only says two things the entire flight.

"We're high, aren't we?"

I reply, "Yup."

Then in a deep, very systematic, slow cadence, he says, "It'll be crazy if something happens up here."

I don't respond to the threat. I just stare at him.

The flight attendant keeps trying to bring us drinks and snacks, and we keep turning her down. When she brings ice cream, my partner can't resist. However, I'm not allowing Hossein to have any, nor do I have any.

During the entire flight, he doesn't eat, doesn't ask to go to the bathroom, and doesn't watch TV. This is rare. When people are taken into custody, most of the time, they become very needy. But Hossein is extremely stoic. This is all business for him. He's not pissed, upset, inquisitive, or argumentative in any way. I can only imagine what he is thinking about. I can't stop thinking about him trying to escape. My mind is running through a thousand "what if" scenarios, and I can't calm my mind down. I finally have him in handcuffs, and I can't screw this up now.

* * *

When we land in Orange County on September 9, 2014, Hossein's absconding charges are automatically dropped. It falls to me to deal with the original crime in the original location so that justice can be served for Mary and Michael.

I charge Hossein and book him with the kidnapping and brutal torture in Newport Beach.

Cortney is elated. Everything feels good. She feels safe and is confident she's done the right thing. She gets a creepy birthday card from Hossein, but she's not dwelling on how he got her address or what the card says. She's moving on with her life.

And so am I.

I'm back to my normal routine at home and routine investigations at work. I'm able to spend more time with my family as a dad, husband, and volunteer coach. I'm getting back in the rhythm of things at church and at home while Hossein's case is getting pushed further and further back on the court docket.

Fine by me, let him wait.

While he's waiting for his day in court, we still have several loose ends to clean up with the rest of the gang. We proffer Naomi, interview Naomi's friend about the van rental, pick up some more evidence, and set our sights on Kyle's jury trial.

In January of 2016, our lives are turned upside down again. I'm at home with my wife and kids when I get a call from one of my best friends, Sergeant Comte. He says the Orange County sheriffs just called the office. "They're looking for you," he says.

"Why are they looking for me?" I ask.

He pauses for an extraordinarily long time.

Hossein has escaped.

* * *

I rocket out of bed and call my boss. That night I go to the command post to help. My family, unfortunately, is scared to death.

The Men's Central Jail is putting together a Department Operations Center to figure out what is going on. This war room of sorts is the hub of all intel, logistics, and investigation. The jail is investigating the escape administratively, while the FBI and marshals department are working together to find Hossein and his newfound friends.

I don't know the negligence that led to him being able to escape. But frankly, that's not my job right now. My job is to conduct interviews and get this guy back behind bars.

My wife is terrified.

* * *

We learn that Hossein Nayeri had been held in module F, a place intended for low-level inmates. Why was he in module F? Why was he given so much freedom? I knew it wasn't up to me to decide, but damn! Moving forward, I knew I had to focus on the present and what we needed to do right now to recapture the guy I hunted for over a year. I couldn't do anything but shake my head and focus on where he was going. While there, he took advantage of a divorcée who teaches inmates English as a second language. The teacher is in the control room, and I'm interviewing her to help figure out what's happening.

What's happened, I ask her? Why am I talking to you? What is it that you know?

"I just felt bad for him. He wasn't getting the resources he deserved. He wasn't getting educated about his case, and that's where I felt it was my duty to help him understand."

That night the sheriff's department serves a warrant on her house and gets a search history on her computer. They find anything that is in public record about his trial. She has found pictures of Cortney, DDA Murphy, DDA Brown, and myself with some of our home addresses and has given them to Hossein. This revelation is shattering. The seven days that follow are pure terror for me and my family, knowing we are possibly Hossein's next targets.

"I thought I was helping him prepare for court. I swear I didn't know he was planning an escape."

I could probably articulate what I was feeling and thinking while this ESL teacher tells me her side of the story, but it wouldn't capture the rage that was going through me.

But back to business.

For all intents and purposes, this is a new investigation. Hossein is loose. For all we know, he's on a mission to hunt down Cortney, myself, and our district's legal team. The teacher swears she is not in contact with Hossein. She promises she's never spoken with the other criminals who escaped with him. She's not charged with anything and is fired.

I have to go in. He knows everything in the court documents. He knows Cortney turned on him and threw him under the bus. He knows I'm the one responsible for his arrest.

A chill washes over the community. We are now on a frantic manhunt. Hossein has a sixteen-hour head start. During the first critical hour of the investigation, we don't know who he escaped with or where he's going. Cortney is our first concern. The Los Angeles County sheriff's department informs Cortney that

Hossein is on the loose. Her worst nightmare is back, and she's afraid for her life. We get her a hotel under a fake name so she can hide out.

I call our police department and dispatch three patrol cars to sit on my house. I notify my wife, who is on edge about these new developments. Even my neighbors are feeling the stress. We also send officers to DDA Matt Murph's house and get DDA Heather Brown to a hotel to get out of the picture and keep her family safe.

We assume Hossein is finding a way to get back to Iran, but he's always relied on Cortney to help him make his escapes in the past. We know he's going to be very angry at all of us because he's read all of the documents that tie us to his case.

Will he harm Cortney?

Are my wife and children safe? How involved should I be? Should I be at home with my family twenty-four hours a day or hunting Hossein?

And . . .

Who are the guys with him? How did he make friends so fast? He doesn't have anyone on the outside.

Where the hell is he going?

* * *

Hossein is not one to do his own dirty work. The inmates that helped him escape are Vietnamese gangsters: Bac Duong, forty-three, and Jonathan Tieu, twenty.

As a first step, they use their contacts and resources on the outside to get Hossein a phone. He starts videotaping himself in jail to document everything.

The videos begin the night before they escape. They show how the inmates create harnesses to climb up ventilation piping until they can reach the trap door to the roof. This means they had access to the roof— and therefore had access to the Vietnamese street gang who brought them materials for their escape— for a couple weeks *before* they escaped.

Eventually, when the time is right, the trio manages to climb down four stories, to the ground, *without being detected*. They get picked up by a few local Vietnamese gangsters, put together by his newfound friends, and then begin hunting Cortney.

They take a ride to Westminster, where they hail a cab. The taxi driver is a Vietnamese immigrant named Long Ma. To him, they seem like regular people hiring a cab.

Long Ma: *I didn't pay it much attention; it's normal. You know, people call me, and I just, you know, pick them up.*

But the three passengers were far from normal. During the car ride to Northern California, they pull a gun on him, take his car key, and take him to a hotel, where they stay for three nights. We later learn that Hossein would sleep with his feet on the chair, blocking the door, so Long Ma couldn't get out. Hossein, Bac, and Jonathan—the three escapees holed up together for three days in a hotel with the cabbie—argue among themselves about whether they should kill Long Ma or not. A falling out among thieves would have been a tame expression for the heated exchange going on in hotel room number 714. The pressure among the escapees is intense and mounting. Bac and Jonathan are not on the same page with Hossein and are becoming frightened.

And there is an interesting side story going on between Bac and Long Ma.

On the fourth morning, Bac has had enough. Bac tells Long Ma that he wants to be accepted as his godson. The two of them sneak out while Hossein and Jonathan are sleeping and take the cab back to Southern California, where Bac turns himself in.

We are lucky and catch a break when we badly need it.

Bac tells us how they kidnapped Long Ma and held him hostage for several days in the hotel. He gives us the full story, agreeing that Hossein is no idiot. In fact, Hossein is so scary that Bac would rather spend his life in jail than be free with Hossein.

He gives us a list of names of people that Hossein wants to find, but I don't recognize any of them. He also tells us the most terrifying information next: where Hossein is going. All of our suspicions are confirmed.

He's trying to find Cortney.

Hossein is seen on a surveillance camera way up north. We're a day behind him. They are looking for Cortney, but they aren't quite on the right trail. There's a girl that lives there who is also named Cortney Shegerian. He got the wrong Cortney and is still forcing Jonathan to help him with his sick plot.

Hossein lacks resources now and is still only in possession of the flip phone given to him by Jonathan Tieu. He struck out once when attempting to locate Cortney and is now lost. The last two times he ran from the law, he had Cortney and Naomi doing his dirty work and providing him money and medication (bipolar meds). But now Naomi is in custody, and Cortney is on the run from him. Subsequently, he's spinning his wheels with nowhere to go. Hossein and Jonathan Tieu are now sleeping in a stolen van, eating miscellaneous groceries, and making vlogs about their endeavors.

* * *

Looking back, I can see I have divulged too much of the information about this case to my wife for her own good—and peace of mind. In real time, while the original crime had unfolded, I told her details of the kidnapping that were now haunting her every day as the national news picks up on the jail escapees.

Ashlee has a first-rate mind and a steel-trap memory. She remembers with great clarity the detail about the assailants—on the day of the crime—breaking in during broad daylight and staying hidden until midnight before the kidnapping. She has a true fear that Hossein could hide inside our house. And so do I. So every time my family and I arrive back at the house after an outing, I do a full search of our home and property while they sit in the car waiting for my "all clear" signal. I systematically go through the house, making sure nothing is suspicious, and verify our safety. And there are unmarked, armed patrol units on our house at all times.

Ash and I start to toss around the idea of going to a hotel. We feel the pressure of our parents who want us safe, and, of course, we feel an obligation to protect our kids. Ash constantly watches her rearview mirror to make sure she isn't being followed in the car, sometimes even intentionally passing our street if she has the slightest suspicion. Every time she gets in and out of the car, she looks around before loading the kids in and out.

While our senses are continually heightened, we don't want to instill that fear into our kids. We feel safe with our 24/7 armed security, and we want to maintain as much normalcy as possible.

We repaint and secure the attic. It seems to help.

There's a national media frenzy going on at this point. The escape is sensationalized on Fox, the Associated Press, CNN, and all major channels. It's starting to feel like a mockery of justice and that Hossein is going to evade the consequences once again—or worse, hurt another person. But the media calling attention to it has been in our favor with one main benefit: We are getting tips on Hossein's whereabouts.

In fact, the leads are good.

An unidentified woman calls in Hossein's location, near the Park District Station in San Francisco. Cops arrive on the scene to find Hossein already on the run. Then, Matthew Hay-Chapman—a homeless resident of the town and a self-described news junkie—has seen Hossein in the local newspaper and is able to point the cops in the right direction.

And they are able to capture Hossein. Again.

Matthew gets a reward from the local DA and a photoshoot with the local news.

We are merely incredibly lucky. Again.

I remember being outside with my family and neighbors when I got the call. We live on a street that is huge on family. There are always a ton of kids playing outside, and the community is close-knit. They know the struggles and rewards of having a cop for a neighbor.

My wife is walking out of the garage toward me. She sees me answer the phone, and she sees a big grin light up my face. Sergeant Darnell, one of my good friends, is on the Orange County Sheriff's apprehension team. It is his voice on the other end of the line.

We've got him. He's in custody.

My wife runs up to me and hugs me through tears of relief. The neighbors are all high-fiving, and the kids are jumping up and down. It is a good moment in the neighborhood.

I had met Sergeant Darnell years prior while coaching our boys' soccer team. We were on the same team a few times, and it is so good to get this call from someone who knows how important this is to me.

Sergeant Darnell drives Hossein down from the San Francisco jail to Orange County.

After eight days, the manhunt comes to an end. The two remaining fugitives are back behind bars. Not surprisingly, they have pleaded not guilty. Back in custody in the same jail he escaped from, Hossein is put on complete lockdown twenty-three hours a day. He can't go anywhere without chains on, and cameras are watching his every move. This case kicks off a huge administrative investigation on the security of the prison.

Up to this point, we have apprehended everyone involved.

Hossein is in Central, waiting to go to trial.

Kyle went to trial first. The jury deliberated for less than two hours before convicting him of kidnapping for ransom, aggravated mayhem, torture, and burglary. Kyle is now in prison, serving two counts of life in prison without parole.

Ryan is also in prison, serving twelve years after he pleads guilty during his plea. Naomi also takes a plea deal and pleads guilty during her trial.

We want a final sentence for Hossein to get closure on this case.

PART V

The Trial

CHAPTER 12

*I*n many ways, I'm the keeper of this story. As lead detective, I've been holding all the key details of this case close to mind since it happened so that I could share them when the time came for a trial. It's critical that I have maintained a crystal-clear picture of what happened on October 2, 2012, for my moments on the stand. And now we've made it to the finish line. A year has gone by after Hossein is apprehended, and we're on our way to court.

I have spent several nights considering proper punishment in preparing for the *voir dire*. As DDA Matt Murphy and DDA Heather Brown and I team up and prepare for trial, I can't go a minute without thinking about what will happen in court. *What is fair for Michael? For Mary? Given the available punishment outlined in the statute, what amount of time could possibly "correct" or atone for these wrongs? What does it take to make things right for the community? Ultimately, how do we stop this from happening again?*

During jury selection, we review the standard questionnaire and ask a few clarifying questions of the potential jurors. Judge Gregg Prickett also asks them questions. One of the jurors says he has major anxiety and smokes weed all day to cope with it. He doesn't want to be part of this case since it's so closely tied to the weed industry. After he's excused, the defense attorney also gets his turn to question the jury pool. Eventually, we all agree upon the twelve best.

We pray and prep all night the day before the trial starts. Our game plan is to show Hossein Nayeri as a violent, controlling man. Our DA's job is to produce the facts and show Hossein's connection to the crime. Hossein is arrogant, and we know he will lose control. So part of our strategy includes getting under his skin.

The people versus Hossein Nayeri begins in July of 2019. Over the next several months, we provide flawless details, charts, and data to the judge and jury.

Day one in the courtroom is a well-orchestrated circus. Cops from every different department are here to see how things will unfold. Media is buzzing. Michael's dad is there. My colleagues, friends, and neighbors also show up and find seats in the back of the courtroom. It's a full house. And it feels intense.

I'm sitting with the district attorney in the front row, one person away from international fugitive Hossein Nayeri. Hossein's mother has flown in from Iran and is sitting right behind me. For the first three days, she chants voodoo curses to take away my ability to speak and to take away my good looks. *Neat.*

Finally, on the fourth day, the bailiff catches her in action and conveys the message that they will kick her out of the courtroom if she doesn't stop hexing me. I have managed to retain my voice, in any case.

I'm constantly aware of Hossein's body language. His energy is dense, collected, and piercing. He's looming and leaning in just a few seats away. Conscious of his every move, I keep thinking when we get down to the end—and he doesn't see a way out—is he going to lose it? *Will he lunge at me? Get one final jab in? Is this thing going to end in a physical altercation?*

During the first few days, all the main characters are called to the stand: CSI, the law enforcement officer who was in the high-speed pursuit with Hossein,

Steve Williams (the deputy who found Mary), and Michael—everyone except Hossein. We are setting the foundation, piecing things together for the jury step-by-step, showing them Hossein Nayeri is the narcissistic, vile, maniacal mastermind behind the entire event.

During the weeks surrounding the trial, I get up at 5:00 a.m. to mentally prepare myself for the day ahead. It's my job to marshal all the facts and to provide all the evidence—both hard evidence and circumstantial. I'm going to my office at the police station before going to the courthouse each day, finding a computer, and focusing on what evidence we need to weave in. Some days I get photos from our server at the station; other days, I bring hard evidence like the glove or the zip ties. Every morning I have a legal pad with me and write down key dates, bullet points, and highlights that will be important for the day ahead.

In addition to being the truth-bearer, it's also my role to take notes during the trial and show our prosecuting attorneys when the cross-examinations are walking the witnesses down the wrong path. We are constantly making course corrections when the jury is being led astray by the defense.

As the trial progresses, the jury is introduced to Hossein, his ex-wife Cortney, his ex-best-friend Kyle, his love interest Naomi, and her ex-husband Ryan Kevorkian. They are beginning to understand the complexity and nuances of these strange couples' connections.

We are also educating the jury on the weed business here in California. We are showing them that Michael is not a bad guy. He's actually a good guy, an upstanding business guy working within the boundaries of the state and federal government statutes. It's very important the jury understands Michael is the true victim here, while the defense tries to portray Hossein as caught in some kind of misunderstood intrigue in the web of the weed industry.

We are keeping very long, very tedious hours. It's mentally exhausting. The entire time Hossein's attorneys are trying to weave lies and suspicions. Their job isn't really to defend their client so much as to sprinkle doubt on everything we are saying. The burden of proof is on us, and they are constantly trying to make the jury second guess us. It's actually pretty laughable, and everyone on the jury sees it this way. *Almost everyone.*

* * *

A few days into the trial, it's revealed that Hossein wants to testify. This is a big no-no because we will paint him into a corner, and he will sound like he is lying. His attorneys argue with him on this. They don't want him up there. But he's getting pissed and wants to speak up for himself. The entire time he's being described as a monster and a puppeteer. Hossein is cocky, controlling, enraged, and getting physically agitated. He's moving around in his chair and can't sit straight.

So when we learn that Hossein is going to get on the stand, the court erupts.

Let's be clear that we aren't worried about him talking. We know this is going to work in our favor. Hossein doesn't have a case. His attorneys try to illustrate that he's already rich—they suggest he doesn't need to kidnap someone to steal money. Hossein, they say, has thousands of dollars stored in the walls of a house in Fresno that no one knows about, not even Cortney. He's a wealthy man who has been taken advantage of and framed; he's not a thug.

Their only angle is that I lied. That's it. That's all they've got. They keep trying to spin the narrative to say I planted Hossein's DNA in the glove, that I've lied under oath and framed an innocent convict.

Here's how it went down on the glove:

Part of our evidence was a photo of one blue nitrile (surgical) glove on the floorboard of Kyle's truck that was used in the kidnapping. When we originally saw that glove, we decided to button the truck up and get it back to the station so CSI could process the truck as well as the glove we found for DNA evidence. When CSI began documenting their discoveries, they found a second blue nitrile glove under the bench seat. They noted this and booked the second glove into evidence.

That's why in the photos, you only see one glove—the first glove we found, which had Hossein's DNA on it. Hossein's team is leading the jury to believe we found no DNA on the glove in the photo, planted his DNA on a second glove, and are late to the party, letting everyone know about the second glove. But from day one of processing the truck, we always had two gloves.

The truth is, we can't process every single thing we find. If we found four gun shells, we would have processed one. If that first one had DNA on it, we would go forward to find the person that matched that DNA. If the first shell didn't have DNA on it, we would start processing each shell one by one. This is clearly explained to the jury, and they get it.

But then Hossein gets on the stand.

The district attorney asks Hossein directly: "Are you saying your glove was planted by Detective Peters?"

Hossein turns to face me. He looks me directly in the eye while answering the DA's question. He says, "It's possible. You tell me."

Nayeri is wearing a baby-blue shirt with a pink and blue tie. He's acting and manipulating. For the most part, the jury sees right through him. Eleven out of the twelve jurors understand what's going on. We have evidence to back up everything we've brought to their attention. They know the truth. But remember, the only strategy Hossein has is to plant doubt. The jurors believed the paperwork trail that I explained under oath. Everyone except juror number nine.

Juror nine is visibly upset for Hossein. She's crying when the prosecutors are really going after him. Her body language is leaning in and disturbed. She's falling under Hossein's spell just like Cortney. Just like Naomi. This is not part of our plan.

Hossein is appearing crazier and crazier over the next few days. He's having many outbursts and rants. He goes off on tangents that have nothing to do with the questions or topics at hand. Out of nowhere, Hossein starts telling the jury that Cortney is lying. He thinks she found out about Naomi and just wants to get back at him for hiding his money in the walls of some house in Fresno that she doesn't have access to.

In another outburst, Hossein exclaims that this is all really Kyle's case. He says that Kyle did it, Kyle got arrested, and the only reason he's here is that Kyle is now trying to throw Hossein under the bus for something he didn't do. He felt he had no allies and that everyone was against him—so that's why he fled to Iran.

Several times the judge has to excuse the jurors, shut down the court, and try to get through to Hossein that his behavior has got to stop. He's only allowed to answer the questions. Everyone is getting sick of his shit.

So at the moment when Hossein is asked about cutting off the penis, it's no surprise that he shows the jury just what kind of sick person he is. DDA Matt Murphy is good—real good. He stares Hossein dead in the eye and blames everything on him. He tells Hossein he knows he cut off Michael's penis, and there is no doubt in his mind. Murphy just wants Hossein to tell him, tell us, how and why he did it to put some closure to this whole thing. Murphy did it; he got under his skin. Hossein narrows his eyes, looks him dead in the face, and says, "You want to know how, how it happened? I'll show you . . . personally."

The court once again erupts, and the judge kicks everyone out.

* * *

Outside of court, there is something that has been bothering me. I remember talking to some of the other detectives about this and then going home and talking to my wife about it.

During lunch breaks or before and after court, the defense would act like they were our best friends. One of them even said, "Hey, don't hate me," right before we started testimony the day he called me a liar on the stand. "No hard feelings; it's all business. Don't take it personally."

How do they separate real life and this? How do they go to sleep at night, knowing what they're about to say is a lie? I get that they're doing their job. I get that they're doing it to win a case and protect their client. Yet they still want me to look at them as if they're some upstanding citizens.

Yeah, I'm going to take it personally that you're calling me a liar. I am who I am. I'm designed for it. How would I not take it personally? I take my job seriously.

Don't get me wrong; the defense attorneys were always respectful. There was always a certain friendliness the prosecution and defense teams had with each other. It was just odd to me. I could never invite one of them over to dinner and pretend that a "tough" day in court where they accused me of lying was just . . . nothing.

* * *

There's a lot of banter on the last day of the trial. We wrap up our closing arguments with eagle eyes on the jury. *Could they flip behind closed doors in deliberation? Could they be swayed?* Yeah, they could.

When you're watching jurors in court, it's like watching a story unfold over live TV. They can't control their physical reactions. You're getting everything in real time. Their body language gives us a sense of where they are emotionally with what's being presented to them.

We designed our entire closing argument completely around juror nine. Originally, we thought she would connect with Cortney because she's around the same age. She didn't come across as having a lot of self-confidence. She didn't seem very independent. We honestly thought juror nine would feel for Cortney through all the domestic violence, feeling alone, being isolated and taken advantage of—but that didn't happen at all.

In closing, the DA is looking directly at juror number nine, talking directly to her with a strong, authoritative Dad-like voice. This backfires.

She doesn't like being looked at or talked to directly. She looks the other way. She shuts down and isn't hearing his words. All she is experiencing is that he's loud, scary, and pissed. We can see she feels that somehow she is the one in trouble. Our argument might have been better heard if he had been looking at the person next to her, so she could lock eyes without being looked at. But we can't go back. Both sides rest. The trial is over now, and we'll just have to wait it out.

* * *

Deliberation is a long, jagged journey. We later learn that within thirty minutes, they vote eleven to one. After two days of discussion around the facts of the case, juror number nine finally decides Hossein Nayeri is guilty of all but one thing— she cannot concede to the charge of mutilation. She says they have reason to doubt that he's the one that did the cutting. The other charges have much more weight, so we're OK with letting that one go.

* * *

Is it possible to be both relieved and terrified at the same time? Hossein Nayeri is found guilty of kidnapping for ransom, inflicting great bodily harm, and torture. This brings a rush of emotion and excitement to the courtroom. This is the moment when we realize Hossein is really going away forever.

And while a good feeling is sinking in that we won the case and the conviction, at the same time, I'm wondering if he's going to lose it one last time.

I turn my chair toward him, anticipating a fight. But he isn't doing anything. He's stone-cold still, probably believing he can get this thing appealed. He looks up at me, and we lock eyes. There's an odd air of respect between us that I can't explain.

It's high fives and hugs as our team heads back to our library. We thank one another for a job well done. We're ready to get back to work and put another criminal out of a job.

Hossein is handcuffed and walked off to prison to start his sentence.

* * *

The next thing we know, Hossein fires his attorney immediately. He is looking for someone who will appeal his case. He went through over a dozen attorneys before he finally found one that was willing to try. The case has been nationally publicized, and there is little chance any attorney can seat a jury that hasn't heard of the case to get an appeal. But Hossein knows he can't be sentenced until his appeal is heard.

Finally, an attorney takes his case. It feels very transparent that she only took the case to move things forward to sentencing.

Hossein's appeal is denied. He's sentenced to multiple life sentences without the possibility of parole. But with Hossein Nayeri, there's always a twist. He's sent to county jail—the same jail he escaped from.

Although our case has been completed, Hossein is still awaiting the escape charge. This is a completely different investigation that I'm not involved in. He needs a different attorney to tackle this one. So he's sitting in jail with two life sentences in front of him, waiting for trial on the escape charge. The jail could probably drop the charges, but they don't want to do that.

They keep pushing the dates off.

* * *

This story started with my role as a SWAT operator, a grunt on the front lines doing the dirty work. And by the end, I'm a SWAT commander, in charge of our swat and negotiation units. There's a shit ton of life that happened to get me here.

After Hossein is found guilty, life feels like it can move forward again—personally and professionally. I get promoted, I'm back coaching football and soccer, and life is good.

I take a SWAT call. It involves domestic violence. A man shoots at his wife. She runs, he's armed, and he barricades himself in the house with a handgun. He misses with the shot he fires at his wife. Next thing that happens, he's in his backyard pointing a gun at a helicopter. He's drunk. He manages to get back to his bunker in the house. He won't come out. We are formulating a plan and negotiating with him for hours. We finally convince him to come out to the front, where we shoot him with a non-lethal 40mm sponge round and then send in a K-9 with a good bite.

The dog gets the glory of taking him into custody.

Truth be told, there are no breaks, no downtime in the world of law enforcement. Even after a successful investigation, apprehension, and ultimate conviction and sentencing, there's always another case to solve. On to the next.

* * *

Q&A SECTION FOR READER

1. If I'm afraid there's someone in my house—what should I do? How do I search the house safely?

   Don't search your own house. Call your local police department and ask them to help out. They'll want to know why you think someone is in your house, i.e., the door was open, the door was kicked open, the back sliding glass door is broken, the screen is off my window, etc. If none of that applies and you're going to search your own house, have

911 ready to go on your phone. Start the search from one section of your house and systematically go through it. Example: Don't skip the downstairs bathroom or closet and then go directly upstairs. Don't start upstairs either. Start downstairs and go from room to room before moving on to the next section.

2.   What was the most difficult part of the case for you to handle, personally? What was your worst moment?

The most difficult part was balancing my emotions in and around my family and friends. There were times I thought they knew too much, but if I didn't give them something, they wouldn't truly grasp where I might be emotionally. Giving some insight into what you're dealing with to your spouse or significant other is healthy, but it walks a fine line if it's too much. Spouses and significant others aren't wired like law enforcement professionals, so they handle the information differently. And being aware of that and working within their cognitive and emotional abilities can be difficult at times.

Some of my worst moments in the case came when I tried to do too much on my own. Cases like this aren't solved by one investigator. I had to rely on and use several detectives throughout this case, and without their support and efforts, this case would not have been successful.

3. It looks like Cortney is going to go free and not pay for her role in this crime. How does that make you feel?

    In many ways, it bothered me at first. I believe at my core that justice is good. Justice is necessary. So to know she wasn't going to face any consequences after this was all over was a difficult pill to swallow. But as time went on, and I got to know Cortney, and know who she was, and know what she's all about, my mind shifted a bit. I know a lot of what she did in life was out of fear. She didn't have any emotional/mental support, and life was difficult. I'm not giving her a pass, and I wouldn't have had she not testified against him, but I believe in doing so, she righted her wrongs. She made sure the true mastermind was in prison. It would have been a much more difficult road had she not stepped up to help.

4. You made a point in the introduction that you had a normal family life. How can you turn off work when it's that intense?

    I know I talk about a "normal" family life in the beginning, but the truth is no law enforcement officer lives a normal life outside of work. There are a few professions where you never turn off work when you go home, and law enforcement is one of them. You do learn, over time, how to manage the level of effort you're putting in. As an example, when I'm at work, my threat level awareness meter is a ten out of ten, but when I'm at the park with my kids, it's a four out of ten. Law enforcement officers can't help but evaluate their surroundings or evaluate the actions of others. We're constantly doing threat assessments because that's what keeps us alive when we're at work. We don't want to be caught slipping.

5. With the current climate for defunding the police and all of the politics, what are some things I can do to support our local police department?

    Support comes in many different forms. We could use the support on social media. You share your police department's local heroics through whichever platform you have, or you can like a certain post. You can also stop by and drop off a few gift cards for a local restaurant or coffee shop. And the best way to support yourself when you're driving around, eating at the local restaurant, or walking your dog is to wave "hi" and say thank you for your service. A smile goes a long way in putting that officer in a good mood while he/she is protecting your streets.

6. Do you still talk to Michael and is he still in the marijuana business?

    I don't talk to Michael or his family anymore. Don't get me wrong; if I saw them on the street, I'd give all of them a big hug and sit and chat for a bit. But I wasn't in their life to be friends. I was in their life to bring justice to their nightmare.

Michael was or is a very good businessman. So I believe Michael is still in the marijuana business. I stopped looking into Michael the day we arrested Hossein. I'm sure the business is still financially lucrative and hard to stop.

7. Did you ever find the penis?

No. I have on very good authority that Hossein made Kyle bring it back with him after they left Michael in the desert. Hossein thought it would make Kyle step up his involvement. Hossein always looked at Kyle as weak, and that was just another way to screw with him. They discarded the penis once they got back to Orange County.

8. Is your family happy about the conviction, and did they know all the details of the case?

They are happy that bad guys are in jail, and that's one less societal threat running around the streets.

They knew as much as I was going to allow them to know. They didn't know all the details and my wife obviously knew more than the kids. They were pretty young when this all took place; they're older now and know a little bit more. But their knowledge of the incident still lacks major detail.

9. You mentioned you were promoted. You also worked SWAT and patrol. What was your favorite position, and why?

Investigative work is by far the most fun. It takes a team—a solid, well-functioning team—and the willingness to take a case to the ends of the earth. Every investigative unit I've worked in was a blast.

The most rewarding, however, has been as a field sergeant. It was incredibly fulfilling to be out in the field with the guys, make a positive impact on the community, and mentor patrol officers.

10. Did you work with DDA Heather Brown or DDA Matt Murphy on any

other big cases, and how was it working with them?

I had the privilege to work with DDA Matt Murphy on a few homicide cases. And it was truly a privilege. There is no doubt in my mind that he was Orange County's best trial attorney (he has since retired). He was smooth, articulate, confident, and fun to watch in trial. When he retired, Orange County lost a good one.

This case was the only time I got to work with DDA Heather Brown, and she, too, was amazing. She was fun to work with, and I loved her attitude. She is a lil fighter and wasn't afraid of anything. She constantly thought outside the box, and there was no such thing as downtime. Her mind was going 100 miles an hour, twenty-four hours a day. She called so often, all hours of the day, that at some point she'd call, and my wife and her would be talking before I even knew Heather called to talk to me. To say she was a tremendous asset to the case would be an understatement.

She's now the big dog inside the DA's office, working on all the big homicides.

ABOUT THE AUTHOR

Ryan Peters began his career in law enforcement in 2001 with the Long Beach, and then Newport Police Departments. With over twenty years of experience, he has worked as a Field Training Officer, SWAT Operator, Robbery/Homicide Detective, Patrol Sergeant, SWAT Team Commander, Internal Affairs Investigator, Robbery Homicide Sergeant, Lieutenant, Area Commander, and Traffic Commander.

www.ingramcontent.com/pod-product-compliance
Lightning Source LLC
Chambersburg PA
CBHW032054040426
42335CB00037B/715